66 Strategies to Program Design
By Stéphane Cazeault

As a strength coach or personal trainer, continuing education is essential.

Simply developing the habit of learning through reading can be beneficial to improving knowledge and ensuring you are at the forefront of training information.

In a 2010 study from the European Journal of Social Psychology, it was established that it takes on average 66 days to create a new habit.[1] If you diligently read and apply one strategy every day for the next 66 days, you will develop and or improve the habit of learning.

This book provides 66 program design strategies to help you as a strength coach or personal trainer refine your programming expertise.

[1] Lally, Phillippa, et al. "How are habits formed: Modelling habit formation in the real world." European journal of social psychology 40.6 (2010): 998-1

Table of Contents

Strategy 1: When training athletes with isometric contractions, it is important to add a dynamic component to allow for proper transfer into speed development

Isometric contractions are very important in athletic development.

However, when training athletes with isometric contractions, it is important to quickly add a dynamic component to allow for proper transfer into speed development, hence the effectiveness of the Stato-dynamic technique.

Here is an example of the Stato-dynamic technique on the Back Squat:

A Back Squat 6 x 4-6 30X2 180

30X2 explained:
- Down on a 3-second count
- On the concentric, you pause right above 90-Degree of knee flexion for a 2-second count
- Finish the concentric with an explosive contraction

The load used for this method is between 60 to 70% of 1RM.

The Stato-dynamic technique is an excellent method to use during the competitive season as it teaches the nervous system to accelerate load from inertia.

Strategy 2: Unilateral exercises are very efficient because they increase neural drive to the muscle, with better neural drive, more muscle fibers get activated for muscular hypertrophy

To compete on a bodybuilding stage, it starts with a good back.

Everyone knows and implements the Chin-up and Pull-up for back, however a great back starts with a strong row.

Here is an example of a rowing exercise progression during a 12-week training cycle designed to increase the hypertrophy of the upper back:

Accumulation 1
A1 One-arm Supinating Seated Row to Waist 3 x 10-12 3011 60

Intensification 1
A1 One-arm Elbow-out Bent-over DB Row 5 x 6-8 4010 90

Accumulation 2
A1 One-arm Bent-over DB Arc Row 4 x 8-10 3011 75

Intensification 2
A1 One-arm Bent-over DB Row 6 x 4-6 3110 120

Notice how all the rowing exercises are unilateral.

The reason unilateral exercises are so efficient is that it increases neural drive to the muscle. With better neural drive, more muscle fibers get activated for muscular hypertrophy.

Strategy 3: With Contrast Training, the higher the training age of the lifter, greater variation in loads are required to create an adequate training response

Contrast Training is a great technique for power development right before the season. Here is a look at a Contrast Training workout former NFL safety, James Butler performed in preparation for training camp:

A1 Deadlift with Chains 5 x 2-4 30X0 10
A2 Triple Jump 5 x 1 X0X0 180

4 reps @ 405 lbs + 60 lb chains of Deadlifts followed directly by triple jumps

Contrast training is a very efficient system to use with high-level athletes. This method is based on the concept of post-tetanic potentiation.

After maximal voluntary contractions (MVC), the nervous system has enhanced motor unit activation properties that can remain elevated for several minutes. The MVC effects can be used effectively for speed-strength training sessions as the improved neuromuscular activation will help recruit high-threshold fibers.

An important consideration with contrast training is that the higher the training age of the lifter, greater variation in loads are required to create an adequate training response.

In the example provided earlier, the load of the Deadlift is at 88% of 1RM followed by a body weight triple jump.

With the compound exercise, the minimum load is 60% of

3

1RM for 3 sets of 5 repetitions, in order to see a post-tetanic effect that will transfer in improved performance of the plyometric exercise.[1]

[1] Smilios, Ilias, et al. "Short-term effects of selected exercise and load in contrast training on vertical jump performance." *The Journal of Strength & Conditioning Research* 19.1 (2005): 135-139.

Strategy 4: Working antagonist movement patterns in double station supersets (A1 and A2) allows for more work done per unit of time as the rest period between exercises can be shortened

Here is a look at a back and shoulders workout of former NFL fullback, Mike Karney:

A1 Chin-Up 4 x 4-6 5010 120
A2 DB Shoulder Press 4 x 4-6 5010 120
B1 Seated Row 3 x 8-10 3011 10
B2 Wide Grip Pulldown 3 x 10-12 4010 120
C1 DB Trap 3 Raise 3 x 12-15 3011 60
C2 DB External Rotation 3 x 12-15 4010 60

In this workout, the A series alternates between a vertical pull and a vertical push movement. Working antagonist movement patterns in double station supersets (A1 and A2) allows for more work done per unit of time as the rest period between exercises can be shortened.

In a single station set-up (one movement only as an A exercise), 6 repetitions would call for a rest period of 3 minutes. By using the antagonist double station, we can now reduce the rest period to 2 minutes.

Let's take a look at both methods:

Single Station
A Chin-up 4 x 4-6 5010 180
B DB Shoulder Press 4 x 4-6 5010 120
Total workout time for both exercises: 29 minutes

Antagonist Double Station
A1 Chin-up 4 x 4-6 5010 120
A2 DB Shoulder Press 4 x 4-6 5010 120
Total workout time for both exercises: 21 minutes

The B series uses a classic Superset method, agonist with agonist without rest in-between. The goal of this superset is to increase the time under tension to the muscle via different motor units.

Even though these are 2 back exercises, the movement patterns are distinct, so different muscle fibers are recruited.

Classic Supersets are a great technique for hypertrophy purposes.
Finally, the program ends with 2 exercises involved in stabilizing the shoulder joint. These exercises are extremely important for joint integrity as well as increasing performance in the major lifts.

Strategy 5: Increased eccentric strength in the brachio-radialis will help alleviate stress off of the elbow during the last portion of the deceleration phase of the throw

When training baseball pitchers, it's important to spend time in the early part of the specific preparation phase strengthening the brachio-radialis. The reason being that increased eccentric strength in this muscle will help alleviate stress off the elbow during the last portion of the deceleration phase of the throw.

Considering that the volume of throwing will rapidly increase during Spring Training, it's important to make sure the throwing elbow will get all the help it needs. A good exercise to implement is the One-arm DB Zottman Scott Curl for 5 sets of 4-6 reps with a 50X0 tempo.

Strategy 6: During a shoulder specialization phase, a good approach is to reduce training volume of the biceps and triceps in order to increase training response

If you are a figure competitor, we all know how important fully developed shoulders are.

To bring up a body part, the training program needs to focus on it.

During a shoulder specialization phase, a good approach is to reduce training volume on biceps and triceps to 4 sets each.

Here is an example of a training split designed to increase shoulder hypertrophy:

Day 1: Back & Shoulders
Day 2: Lower Body
Day 3: Arms & Shoulders
Day 4: Off

Repeat...

This is an example of the Arms & Shoulders session:

A1 Lean-away DB Lateral Raise 4 x 10-12 2010 10
A2 One-arm DB Lateral Raise 4 x 10-12 2010 10
A3 30-Degree Sidelying DB Lateral Raise 4 x 10-12 2010 10
B 15-Degree Prone DB Lateral Raise 3 x 12-15 2012
C1 Incline DB Curl 4 x 8-10 3012 75
C2 Decline DB Triceps Extension 4 x 8-10 5010 75

The A1, A2, and A3 exercises are done back to back. Start

with the weaker side from A1 to A3, before doing the other arm from A1 to A3 again. Keep going back and forth between the left and right side until all 4 sets are completed.

Strategy 7: A simple, yet effective progression to improve deadlift strength is starting the training cycle with long range of motion deadlift variations and progressing by reducing the pulling distance

Here is a simple, yet effective progression to improve deadlift strength.

The first phase emphasizes Structural Balance with more isolated work for the spinal erectors. The following phase uses long range of motion for the deadlift by doing Snatch-grip Podium Deadlift, followed by Snatch-grip Deadlift on Floor for the third phase and finally regular Clean-grip Deadlifts on the last phase of the Cycle.

Give this progression a try if you're looking for a quick improvement in your Deadlift strength.

Q: What isolated work for the spinal erectors did you do? And I assume that was the client's weak link in the posterior chain?
A: Specifically, the client did some Stiff-legged Deadlifts and Wide Stance Seated Goodmornings. You're right as far as the weak link, I feel that most people are weak in the bottom-end of the strength curve of the hip extensors (which is why I love Goodmornings) and also, I like these two exercises to help with flexibility to prepare for the increased range of motion of the Snatch-Grip Deadlift on Podium.

Q: How long are each of the phases?
A: 3 weeks

Strategy 8: When training the energy systems, it is important to understand that the muscle fibers used in the chosen exercise have to be specific to actions of the sport

When training the energy systems, it's important to understand that the muscle fibers used in the chosen exercise have to be specific to the sport.

Football players will only get more efficient at sprinting by running and focusing on acceleration. For example, biking and rowing would be cross-training, cross-training would help a little, but they still need to sprint. The sequence of firing must be specific. The cross-training effect will be working the heart and lungs, but only the specific muscle fibers used in the sport will become efficient at clearing lactic acid.

A solid method for training the energy systems with football players is short Prowler accelerations (5-10 meters) followed by sprints. This mimics the initial acceleration phase and load of pushing away defenders with breakaway speed.

Strategy 9: One of the keys to program design is to always put the highest velocity exercise first in the training program

Here is an example of a lower body workout from the first accumulation phase of a 12-week power training cycle.

This is the full workout:
A Hang Clean 5 x 4-6 10X0 120
B Front Squat 8,8,6,6,4,4 30X0 180
C Glute Ham Raise 4 x 6-8 30X0 120
D Hanging Leg Raise 4 x 12-15 30X0 120

One of the keys to program design is to always put the highest velocity exercise first in the training program.

Strategy 10: Eccentric contractions are the trigger to muscle growth, once a trainee gets accustomed to slower eccentrics, you can further the hypertrophy process by using slow eccentrics at the end of a set

Almost 30 years ago research demonstrated that eccentric contractions were the trigger to muscle growth. For this reason, when first starting to train a client it is good to introduce a 4010 tempo to their training program. It teaches the athlete to control the eccentric component of the lift. Once the trainee gets accustomed to this lifting speed you can further the hypertrophy process by using slow eccentrics at the end of a set. For this progression, a solid method is the 4ı2, which works very well for arm development.

You do 4 reps to failure, and then you cheat the weight up and lower the weight for a 10 second count and try to get 2 of these slow eccentric reps. This method allows you to combine two important factors of hypertrophy, load and time under tension. The 4+2 allows you to use a load of 88% of 1RM, which is a relative strength load, but the two eccentric reps add time under tension, putting you in the hypertrophy strength quality.

Strategy 11: When doing a high frequency and high-volume phase, you get 30% better recovery from training 5 days in a row followed by 2 days off

When doing a high-frequency and high-volume phase (two-a-day training), you get 30% better recovery from training 5 days in a row with 2 days off, rather than having 2 days off spread out during the week. This point becomes even more valuable when improvements in performance are the goals of the training program.

3-Week Periodization Matrix

Monday	Tuesday	Wednesday	Thursday	Friday	Saturday	Sunday
Chest & Back	Lower Body	Arms & Shoulders	Posterior Chain	Chest & Back	Off	Off
Chest & Back	Lower Body	Arms & Shoulders	Posterior Chain	Chest & Back	Off	Off
Lower Body	Arms & Shoulders	Off	Chest & Back	Posterior Chain	Off	Off
Lower Body	Arms & Shoulders	Off	Chest & Back	Posterior Chain	Off	Off
Arms & Shoulders	Lower Body	Chest & Back	Posterior Chain	Arms & Shoulders	Off	Off
Arms & Shoulders	Lower Body	Chest & Back	Posterior Chain	Arms & Shoulders	Off	Off

Q: Can you elaborate on the Wednesday off day in week 2?

A: It is logistics. If you notice the frequency per body parts in this 3-week phase, for the upper body you have 8 days (16 sessions) and for the lower body you have 6 days (12 sessions), so it is 14 days of training to fit in a 15-day bracket. By using the week 2 Wednesday, you add the off day righ tin the middle of the phase.

Strategy 12: An Incomplete Recovery Functional Hypertrophy rep scheme is an effective training method for Endurance Athletes during the Specific Preparation Phase

Endurance based sports attract a lot of confusion on a weight-training program design perspective. It seems logical at first glance to write a weight-training program that favors Strength Endurance, but it may be somewhat redundant considering the immense volume of endurance work they do practicing their sport. To this effect, alternate between phases of Hypertrophy and Functional Hypertrophy during the General Preparation Phase to help regain lost hypertrophy during the competitive season, as well as focusing on bringing up body parts that might have been underused during their sports practice.

As you get into the Specific Preparation Phase, switch the focus of the alternating periodization between phases of Functional Hypertrophy and Relative Strength. This allows the athlete to maintain a healthy level of functional muscle mass for the rigors of the season, but also allows for superior strength levels.

It's important to know that strength is the mother of all strength qualities, with everything else being equal, a stronger athlete will always perform at a higher level.

One particular method that I find very effective during the Specific Preparation Phase is the use of an incomplete recovery Functional Hypertrophy rep scheme.

Here is an example:

A Pull-up 5 x 7 3010 90

16

With this set-up, assuming a 1RM of 100kg, loading would look like this:

Set 1: 7 @ 80kg

Set 2: 7 @ 78kg

Set 3: 7 @ 75kg

Set 4: 7 @ 73kg

Set 5: 7 @ 70kg

Because of the accumulative fatigue created by the shorter rest period, the athlete will need to decrease the load by 2-3% with each set. It is important to note that this system works better with advanced lifters, as weaker athletes will often have enough rest with 90 seconds at this rep range. The advantages of using this method with an endurance athlete in the Specific Preparation Phase is that on top of improving strength and hypertrophy (because you're staying above the minimum strength threshold of 70% of 1RM), you are also improving Anaerobic Lactic Capacity, which is the key to performance in endurance sports.

Strategy 13: Plyometric training is the fastest of all training modalities, for this reason, the best way to progress is by training it in a rested state

Plyometric training is one of the most misunderstood aspects of strength and conditioning. Too often we see athletes undergo extensive plyometric sessions year round. The problem is that in-season, the athlete is already doing a lot of plyometric work playing their sport. Adding more explosive work to the training week can become rather ineffective as the CNS will fatigue to a point of diminishing return.

The key factor of plyometric work is to focus on quality over quantity. Plyometric training is the fastest of all training modalities, for this reason, the only way you will progress is by training it in a resting state. Cumulative fatigue will not only inhibit progress but may even lead to a regression in performance.Even though in some cases plyometric work can be trained year round if well planned, a good approach is training it during the off-season and for no longer than 12 weeks.

In a training phase, a good approach is adding 2 Plyometric sessions per week. It is imperative to understand that the goal is to create as short a ground contact time as possible. Quality of work is so important that sets of approximately 20 seconds maximum should be used. The training effect of Plyometric training is very specific; it's better to do more sets of fewer exercises rather than few sets of multiple exercises.

Strategy 14: Normally, the B series should be slightly lower in intensity than the A series

Here is an example of an upper body workout from the first accumulation phase of a 12-week power training cycle.

This is the full workout:
A1 Standing Overhead Press 8,8,6,6,4,4 30X0 90
A2 Neutral-grip Chin-up 8,8,6,6,4,4 30X0 90
B1 Dip 8,8,6,6,4,4 30X0 90
B2 Prone T-bar Row 8,8,6,6,4,4 30X0 90

One important program design note with this workout is that normally you want the B series to be of a slightly lower intensity (higher reps) than the A series, but sometimes it is good to challenge the lifter by overloading with the same rep scheme in the B series.

Strategy 15: Periodizing training priorities is important when improving a lift because you can't always hammer the same lift over and over again

The Front Squat is a great exercise for the lower body, but the focus of this strategy is not really about the Front Squat.

One of my online clients completed three 12-week training cycles. Initially, the goal was to improve his Back Squat. The first cycle was focused on Back Squat, then the second cycle we switched the focus to the Deadlift, to finally come back to the Back Squat in the 3rd cycle.

When improving a lift, unfortunately, you can't always hammer the same lift over and over again; hence why cycling the priorities is important. Now, the problem is that during the three 12-week cycles, the Front Squat was not touched once. For this reason, the training cycle that followed focused on the Front Squat.

The client's Front Squat was good considering it was his first exposure in over a year. Our goal was a Front Squat of 300 lbs. At first, he completed 4 reps at 185 lbs which is a 1RM equivalent of 210 lbs. This means that the client was working at 70% of his target goal. Understanding that on average, a lifter can gain about 2-3% strength per workout; we knew that by the time we finished this phase, we would need 4 more 3-week phases to reach the goal. But, progress is not linear, we could not have him blast away Front Squats continuously for 18 more workouts and expect he'd reach a 1RM of 300 lbs by that time.

For this reason, the 4 phases would be split by adding a 12-week cycle focusing on the Deadlift. The good thing about the Deadlift is that the strength gained in the lower back tends to improve Front Squat poundages. With all this said, we were confident that the client would reach the 300 lbs Front Squat goal within 24 weeks. Numbers don't lie.

Q: What would happen if all you did was hammer the front squat?
A: Strength progression would slow down or even stop.

Strategy 16: In order to recruit more motor units, you need to undergo training phases of higher intensities

As a trainee, you can increase muscle size by improving myofibrillar hypertrophy (size of muscle fiber) or sarcoplasmic hypertrophy (fluid in the muscle cell). Both components have their place for complete muscle development. The limiting factor with sarcoplasmic hypertrophy is the nutritional and hormonal status of your athlete. If they are not at adequate levels in both nutrition and hormones, the gains will be limited.

For long-term development, focusing more on improving myofibrillar hypertrophy is a good approach. A classic hypertrophy intensity of 70-75% of 1RM will do just that.

German exercise physiologist Jurgen Hartmann and Harold Tunnemann demonstrated that hypertrophy training does increase the size of the fibers, but does not increase the amount of motor units recruited. In order to recruit more motor units, you need to undergo training phases of higher intensities (85-100% of 1RM). By implementing this information into a properly periodized program is where you can get an edge for mass development.

In short, alternating between phases of hypertrophy (accumulation) and strength (intensification) will yield to better results in the long run because you progressively develop the ability to recruit more muscle fibers to hypertrophy when you get back to your accumulation phases.

Strategy 17: By implementing direct arm work in your training routine, you will become much more efficient in the big compound lifts of the upper body

Direct arm work is often neglected or even avoided by female trainees. It is true that the majority of training time should be spent on multi-joint and metabolically demanding exercises like the Deadlift, the Squat, the Chin-up, and the Bench Press, but often, paying more attention to strengthening the arms can accelerate progress on the Chin-up and Bench Press.

On Chin-ups, strong biceps will assist during the pull and especially during the last part of the movement, as you get closer to the top. With the Bench Press, strong triceps will have a tremendous impact on your ability to push a heavier weight and even more so if you are an athlete with a narrow clavicle and long arms.

By implementing direct arm work in your training routine, overtime you will become much more efficient in the big compound lifts of the upper body. Two exercises to use when introducing direct arm work with a client who rarely trains arms is the Incline Dumbbell Curls for biceps and the Seated EZ-bar French Press for triceps. What is particularly interesting with these exercises is the training effect of more motor unit recruitment caused by training the movements with the muscles in a stretched position.

Strategy 18: One limiting factor with grip is endurance; use a system that builds a progressively longer time under tension from phase to phase

Grip strength is very important in hockey; it allows for more accurate puck handling, harder slap shots and a better chance of winning a fight. The fact is that most of the time the winner of a hockey fight is the one who can hold onto the opponent the longest and with the most control. There are many different ways a strength coach can help an athlete develop a stronger grip, but let's take a look at one way to implement grip training during the off-season with high-level hockey players.The off-season will vary anywhere from 8 to 12 weeks depending on how deep in the playoffs their team went. NHL off-season is one of the shortest in pro sports, for this reason, it is good to use a very systematic and specific approach to grip training.

An example of an off-season training split to use with hockey players is:

Day 1: Arms
Day 2: Legs
Day 3: Off
Day 4: Torso
Day 5: Off

On Day 1, after training arms, do specific work for the grip. Here is a typical progression for the C series to use for Phase 1, 2 and 3 of the entire training cycle:

Phase 1
C1 Pinch Cylinder (Big) 3 x 4-6 1016 60
C2 Pinch Hub 3 x 4-6 1016 60

Phase 2
C1 Pinch Cylinder (Medium) 3 x 6-8 1016 60
C2 Pinch Block (Small) 3 x 6-8 1016 60

Phase 3
C1 Pinch Block (Big) 3 x 8-10 1016 60
C2 Pinch Card 3 x 8-10 1016 60

It is important to notice that one limiting factor with grip is endurance, for this reason, use a system that builds a progressively longer time under tension from phase to phase. Opposite to a normal linear periodization progression that goes from volume to intensity, with grip, use a training sequence that builds towards increasing training volume.

Another important point is to create a contrast from the C1 to the C2 exercise. You go from a really thick implement to a smaller implement, but as you progress to phase 2, you create a smaller contrast to help adapt with the longer time under tension until you finally try to create the biggest contrast from extra thick to extra thin implements. To do so assures maximal adaptations as far as motor unit recruitment for grip strength.

Strategy 19: In order to gain strength on a lift, there is a minimum rep threshold that needs to be reached to create a training effect

The Chin-up is a great upper body exercise, but unfortunately many struggle at progressing on this lift. Many factors can contribute to poor Chin-up performance, but there is one very important aspect that is an often forgotten in programming.

To gain strength on a lift, there is a minimum rep threshold that needs to be reached to create a training effect. Ideally, that rep threshold is around 25 reps (18 being the absolute minimum). For example, if the training program asks for 5 sets of 6 reps, that is 30 reps which is great; but the reality with someone who has a weak Chin-up is the reps will look like this:

Set 1: 6 reps
Set 2: 4 reps
Set 3: 3 reps
Set 4: 2 reps
Set 5: 2 reps

The total number of reps is 17, which is on the low side; and the problem is that the training effect will be minimal by the time the athlete gets back to the next Chin-up workout. A better approach for that trainee would be to do multiple sets of lower reps. By looking at the rep distribution of the previous scenario, it is safe to say that 3 reps is probably a realistic number of reps that could be repeated over multiple sets. With that in mind, this athlete should be programmed 8 sets of 3 reps for a total amount of 24 reps. This simple change in program design can make the difference between results and no results on improving the Chin-up.

Q: Is 18 the general rule for all lifts or is it different? I see for example 5,4,3,2,1 method only has 15, so would you need B1 to also be the same exercise to make up for the volume?

A: 18 reps is an absolute minimum but not an optimal number. It is a general number for most lifts.

You are completely right with the 5,4,3,2,1 method only having 15 total reps. It's important to understand that the 5,4,3,2,1 method is more of a Peaking system. You want to use lower volume methods when the demands for very high intensities are warranted in a periodized plan. You would use these methods as a CNS unloading phase leading to a competition. The lower volume will allow the CNS to respond optimally to a high intensity stress, but you can't expect the same level of strength improvement over the long run with these methods.

When you look at all the popular sets and reps scheme you quickly realize that they are all around that 25 rep mark:

3 x 10
4 x 8
5 x 6
5 x 1/1/1/1/1 (Cluster)
6 x 4
7 x 4
8 x 3
3,2,1,3,2,1,3,2,1
10 x 3

Q: I've seen a few articles and videos for progressing in the pull up when someone cannot perform 1 rep with slow tempos, but what with be a minimal volume threshold for that scenario?

A: With slow tempos the volume is gained via TUT, and because long eccentric contractions create more muscle damage, the total volume doesn't have to be as high.

The appropriate set to rep threshold with eccentric work depends on the athletes capacity to tolerate eccentric work, which is a function of the strength deficit of the trainee.

But to answer your question, as a rule of thumb for someone who can't do a single rep on Chin-up, you want to use a set and rep scheme that will allow you a total eccentric TUT of anywhere between 60 to 120 seconds.

In the end, the principle is the same, If you're doing 1 rep on a 10 second eccentric, you'll need more sets to get a training effect than if you're doing 4 reps with a 10 second eccentric.

Q: A lot of longer armed athletes have a difficult time achieving full ROM on chins (deltoid or sternum to the bar). Other than ISO holds at the top, are there any accessory exercises you can suggest to improve this deficiency?
A: Other than Iso Holds you can also do 1 1/4 reps at the top. As far as accessory work, assuming there are no scapular retraction mobility limitations, I like to add some scapular retraction work with different rowing variations using a pause a the top position.

Furthermore, I like to incorporate biceps work emphasizing mostly the end-range (Spider Curl) but also the bottom range (Scott Curl) as it assists to a more powerful first pull increasing momentum to finish the rep.

Strategy 20: When designing a program for strength development, try to find ways to promote training longevity and avoid injuries

When designing a training program, exercise selection is one of the most important training parameters for the success of the training plan. A great Pull-up variation is the Subscapularis Pull-up. To do this variation optimally, you need to be proficient at performing a regular Pull-up. The subscapularis is a muscle that originates behind the scapula and inserts at the head of the humerus. This muscle primarily helps with internally rotating the humerus. When designing a program for strength development, try to find ways to promote training longevity and avoid injuries.

An exercise to develop strength in the extensors of the upper body is the Dip. A strong Dip will carry over to many exercises. One of the issues with Dips is the high amount of tension it creates on the shoulder joint in the bottom position, but we believe in trainees always favoring full range of motion when training.This is when the Subscapularis Pull-up becomes important in the training program. A strong subscapularis muscle will also help protect the shoulder joint by stabilizing the head of the humerus.For this reason, when planning a heavy phase for Dips, pair it with the Subscapularis Pull-up in an attempt to aid with the health of the shoulders.

Q: Would the lean away chin-up be as effective as an alternative to this exercise?
A: Not as much because the humerus goes in slight external rotation during a chin-up.

Q: What are your thoughts on using the pulldown bar in either a neutral or wide grip as a regression from this for people who don't necessarily have chin up proficiency? As an alternative

29

way to functionally strengthen the subscap?
A: I like it a lot. I use the Subscapularis Pulldown all the time with clients who can't do Pull-ups.

Q: Any suggestions for someone who struggles with dips due to a previous AC separation?
A: You can do slow-eccentric only Dips supersetted with Decline Neutral-grip DB Press.

Strategy 21: Pay attention to the way the weight progression of a lift evolves during a training phase in case you need to back off from that lift to let the CNS recharge

Previously we examined the first workout of an online client's training phase, doing 3 reps at 95 kg (209 lbs) on the Deadlift (refer to Strategy 7). The results of the Deadlift for the 3 workouts of the 5,3,5,3,5 wave loading phase went like this:

Session 1:
avg weight 89.4 kg
avg reps 4.2
avg 1RM 101.4 kg
tonnage 1865 kg

Session 2:
avg weight 94 kg
avg reps 4.2
avg 1RM 106.6 kg
tonnage 1960 kg

Session 3:
avg weight 98.3 kg
avg reps 3.3
avg 1RM 107.7 kg
tonnage 1242 kg

By looking at the numbers, we can see that the average 1RM went up 6.3 kg (13.9 lbs), which is positive during an Intensification phase as the load is the definite measure of intensity. When you look closely, we can see a 5.2 kg improvement from session 1 to session 2, but only a 1.1 kg improvement from session 2 to session 3. Furthermore, even

31

though this is mostly a measure of volume, the tonnage on the Deadlift increased 5% from session 1 to 2, which is better than average, but dropped 37% from session 2 to 3.

The high level of fatigue that set in prevented the client from performing the last set of 5. To summarize, when seeing a lift evolve in this fashion during a training phase, it gives you a clear message that you need to back off from that lift to let the CNS recharge. That 5,3,5,3,5 wave loading phase was the last training cycle. Next will be a completely new cycle with an accumulation phase where the average intensity will drop by 15%. No Deadlifts will be performed, but rather attacking the posterior chain muscles throughout the entire spectrum of the strength curve.

Strategy 22: When a plateau in mass gain occurs, use a method that will create a completely different stimulus to the muscle and nervous system

A very important aspect of the hypertrophy process is creating a disturbance in homeostasis. When a plateau in mass gain occurs, it's a good idea to use a method that will create a completely different stimulus to the muscle and nervous system.

An approach to programming that is very efficient at shocking the body for hypertrophy is creating extreme variations in tempo prescription. Here is an example of a Lower Body workout using this method:

A1 Heel Elevated Squat 5 x 3-5 5010 120
A2 Lying Leg Curl 5 x 3-5 5010 120
B1 Heel Elevated Squat 4 x 3-5 5050 90
B2 Lying Leg Curl 4 x 3-5 5050 90
C1 Heel Elevated Squat 3 x 3-5 5550 60
C2 Lying Leg Curl 3 x 3-5 5055 60

This workout will do many things in helping the hypertrophy response:

1) Keeping the same exercises throughout the entire session will create a huge demand on the muscle fibers by causing repeated exposure to the same motor pattern.

2) The fibers will go through the entire spectrum of hypertrophy, from high-end Functional Hypertrophy at 30 seconds TUT to classic Hypertrophy at 50 seconds TUT and finally low-end Endurance at 75 seconds TUT. This range in set duration allows for complete fatigue of the type IIx and IIa

33

fibers with some fatigue of the IIb fibers in the A series.

3) A slower eccentric tempo creates more muscle damage and increases the output of IGF-1.

4) A slower concentric tempo increases intra-muscular tension which along with TUT is a key component of hypertrophy.

5) Isometric contractions allow for greater fiber recruitment and tension.

Give this workout a try if you feel a change of pace is warranted during a hypertrophy cycle.

Strategy 23: An important program design consideration is to use the Behind-the-neck Press during an Accumulation phase when the intensity is lower

Back & Shoulders are two muscle groups that pair very well together. Pairing a vertical pull and vertical push in the A series is a very natural combination.

Let's examine an A series of an online client:

Accumulation 4
Day 1: Back & Shoulders
A1 Sternum Chin-up 6 x 4-6 3011 90
A2 Seated Behind-the-neck Press 8,6,4,4,6,8 4010 90

These two exercises are advanced variations of the Chin-up and Shoulder Press.

To properly execute a Sternum Chin-up, you need to be proficient at regular Chin-ups. What makes this exercise challenging is that as you are starting the pull, you need to push your torso backward to the extent where your lower sternum or upper abdomen will be touching the bar. Thick technique puts tremendous tension on the entire upper back and adding a pause in the contracted position emphasizes the training effect.

The Seated Behind-the-neck Press is a great exercise that lost its popularity in the 90's. It used to be a staple of old-time bodybuilders and strength athletes. The negative over this exercise is that it creates a lot of discomfort on the shoulder joint. An important distinction to understand is that a pre-existing shoulder issue (injury or lack of mobility) will lead to discomfort, but it is not the Behind-the-neck Press that leads

35

to shoulder issues. Before you program the Behind-the-neck press in a workout, make sure the trainee has healthy shoulders. When performed properly, this exercise will work all heads of the shoulders and the strength gains will transfer to most major upper body pressing exercises.

An important program design consideration is to use the Behind-the-neck Press during an Accumulation phase when the intensity is lower. Doing so allows the introduction of the exercise to a more manageable rep scheme, enabling the trainee to cope with the more pronounced external rotation of the shoulders.

Strategy 24: Stronger neck extensors can help with overall strength gains

The neck is an area that is often neglected in training. The reality is that stronger neck extensors can help with overall strength gains. It helps with strength indirectly by improving postural alignment. In fact, simply activating the neck extensors will improve neural drive.

An effective way to train the neck extensors is by implementing neck supports to your training program. Use a standing position and push the back of the head into a Swiss Ball while keeping the chin tucked in and the head aligned with the neck.

In a periodized plan, a good time to incorporate direct work for the neck extensors is during a Structural Balance phase when you are trying to correct muscle imbalances and work on specific weaknesses.

There are many different ways to program neck extensor exercises in a workout, but an effective way to do so is in a superset fashion along with the lower traps.

Here is an example:

A1 Standing Neck Support on Ball 3 x 6-8 1016 10
A2 Prone Trap-3 Raise 3 x 10-12 3011 90

By starting with the Neck Support on Ball, the activation of the neck extensors will create enhanced neural drive, which will potentiate the performance on the Prone Trap-3 Raise.

Q: What's your opinion on using the Harness that hangs off your head for neck training? Is it too much?

A: It is a very useful tool. Try it attached to a low-pulley for even better results.

Strategy 25: When an athlete performs a lot of overhead movements in their sport, favoring exercises that strengthen the scapular-retractors will greatly benefit them

Gymnastics movements are very popular these days and for obvious reasons. The exercises performed are extremely functional and can provide a great base for strength and mobility.

A lot of the movements performed have a high demand for overhead work (Hanging Pulls, Levers, Hand Stance, etc.), but scapular-retractor work can often be neglected in programming. One important side effect of poor scapula-retractor strength is shoulder instability.

When an athlete performs a lot of overhead work in their sport and has some shoulder issues, favoring exercises that strengthen the scapular-retractors will greatly help the athlete.

Let's take a look at the primary scapular-retractor exercises used in the first 2 phases of one of my online clients.

Accumulation 1
Upper Body 1
B1 One-arm DB Arc Row 3 x 8-10 3011 75
Upper Body 2
B1 One-arm Elbow-out DB Row 3 x 8-10 3011 75

Intensification 1
Upper Body 1
B1 One-arm DB Row 8,8,6,6 3110 90
Upper Body 2
B1 One-arm Supinating-grip Seated Row 8,8,6,6 3011 90

We can notice the use of only unilateral exercises. Unilateral training can increase neural drive to the prime mover, which is great when trying to improve strength quickly.

In the Accumulation, the first exercise has the arm close to the body to create less strain on the shoulder joint. After neural engagement occurred in workout one, you can progress to a more challenging exercise on the shoulders by doing a rowing movement with the arm away from the body.

In the Intensification phase, using two exercises with the elbows close to the body will be less stressful to the shoulder joint when exposing the trainee to higher intensities (6RM) for the first time.

Simply put, you want to strengthen the scapula-retractors as much as you can while creating the least amount of stress on the joint as possible, but you still need to challenge it once in awhile.

Finally, the primary exercises described in these workouts are in the B series only because the A series is dedicated to remedial work like the trap-3 and the external rotators of the shoulders.

Strategy 26: With speed, intensity is more important than volume

When training for speed development, always consider the importance of the CNS. To optimize the training effect, always train speed in a recovered state. With speed, intensity is more important than volume.

When looking at your periodization during the Specific Preparation Phase, you need to make certain you spend time developing maximal speed before you aim at improving speed-endurance.

For maximal speed, start the session with the shortest distance and gradually increase it within the workout.

10 M x 6
20 M x 5
40 M x 4

For speed-endurance, begin the session with the longest distance and as the athlete fatigues, reduce the distance. This method will give you a higher total intensity by the end of the workout.

80 M x 5
40 M x 4
20 M x 3
10 M x 2

As a coach, the way you oversee the training session is by examining the drop-off in speed performance. The first sprint of the workout determines the pace. Once performance decreases too much from the starting pace, you move on to a shorter distance. For example:

200 M in 30 seconds
200 M in 31 seconds
200 M in 32 seconds
200 M in 33 seconds… pace is too slow; move on to a shorter distance.

100 M in 15 seconds
100 M in 16 seconds
100 M in 17 seconds… pace is too slow; move on to a shorter distance

50 M in 8 seconds
50 M in 9 seconds… pace is too slow; terminate the session.

What happens is once the running pace slows down past a certain point, the nervous system learns to become slower as you are teaching your CNS to recruit lower threshold motor units. Practically speaking, you are better off covering your 30-second 200 M with two 100 M sprints at a 15 second pace, than to keep going on the 200's at a slower pace.

By using this programming strategy, your overall training session intensity (measured by speed) will be at a higher level.

Q: If you're getting too slow at the same distance, is it that the nervous system is getting too fatigued or the muscles?
A: This is like a "chicken or the egg" type of question. The reality is that it depends on the training level of the athlete and also the magnitude of the load of his training week.

What it means is that a well-trained athlete in speed development will have the CNS capacity to withstand repeated high-intensity efforts in the Anaerobic Alactic system, but over time will have diminished recovery of the ATP-CP substrates so the "muscle" will become a limiting factor.

On the other hand, this same athlete could be in a training phase where the weight training programs are Strength and Power based, which impairs his CNS recovery, hence affecting his ability to undergo repeated efforts of high intensity sprints. In this case, the CNS will be a limiting factor.

Strategy 27: When looking to build transferable strength and function with athletes, the focus should be towards an Olympic style Back Squat

The Back Squat is a key lower body exercise when trying to improve lower body strength and power. When looking to build transferable strength and function with athletes, the focus should be towards an Olympic style Back Squat.

A Powerlifting style Back Squat can allow a trainee to use greater loads compared to the Olympic style Back Squat. Nevertheless, a hip hinge Squat can exert up to 11 times more hip torque than a Squat style favoring a forward movement of the knees. That stress at the hip joint can become a problem with athletes in which the sport demands extensive stop-and-go accelerations and change of directions. Over time, the overall stress can lead to injury in which the risk-reward might not be warranted.

Another advantage of the Olympic style Back Squat with athletes is the full range of motion at the knee joint. By going to a full range of motion, you allow for the co-activation of both the quadriceps and hamstrings, leading to better knee joint integrity under load via a more balanced lower body musculature.

For most sports, a strong and powerful movement executed throughout its entire range of motion will not only reduce the risk of injury but also aid in athletic prowess.

Strategy 28: When an athlete struggles with Squat execution, utilize a regressive progression in your athlete's programming

The Back Squat is perceived as the king of lower body exercises, but the reality is that a lot of people struggle with proper squatting mechanics.

When an athlete struggles with Squat execution, as a coach, you need to impose a regressive progression to your athlete's programming.

The most common lagging traits when squatting are ankle mobility, proper knee tracking, hip mobility issues due to length-tension discrepancies with the hip flexors concomitant with poor erector spinae strength and finally, pure biomechanic restrictions created by femur-to-hip joint bone integrity.

The most practical way to remedy the situation as a strength and conditioning coach is to undergo an extensive strength training cycle of Split Squats.

There are many variations of Split Squat progressions one can use for Squatting success but here is a particularly effective 12-week progression for power athletes:

Accumulation 1
A1 DB Split Squat, 1 1/4 reps 3 x 8-10 4010 60

Intensification 1
A1 DB Split Squat 4 x 5-7 3110 90

Accumulation 2
A1 BB Split Squat, Double Barrel 1 1/4 reps 3 x 6-8 3010 75

45

Intensification 2
A1 BB Split Squat 5 x 4-6 3010 90

By using this progression, your athlete will improve ankle mobility, knee tracking, and hip flexibility through different time under tensions and technical modalities. An important factor with programming Split Squats is that since this exercise is classified as an assistance exercise, the lowest amount of reps prescribed is 6.

In most cases, following this progression should allow your athlete to perform a proper full range of motion Back Squat without any energy leaks due to poor biomechanics.

Q: How would this look in a program? As in how many days a week would you be doing each exercise?

For example, would you do Accumulation 1 on Day 1 then Intensification on day 2 or would you do Accumulation 1 for the first three weeks then move on to Intensification for the next three and so on?
A: Twice a week for 3 weeks and then move on to the next phase for 3 weeks, etc.

Q: Would there be much change in front and back foot elevations?
A: With someone very tight, you could start with front foot elevated, then front foot flat, then rear foot elevated and finally back to front foot flat.

Q: Just curious why you started with 1 1/4 rep split squat?
A: To increase time under tension in the weakest part of the movement. Doing so will increase VMO recruitment as well as increase the exposure to the stretch of the hip flexors.

Q: Since the 1 1/4 is an advanced progression – is it ok to start off with 1 1/4 instead of just regular split squats?
A: It is more of an advanced progression, but keep in mind that the progression in this example referred to athletes. In most cases they will do fine with starting with a 1 1/4 technique. Whenever a client can handle it, the results will come quicker. That being said, with general population I would not use 1 1/4 right away.

Strategy 29: It is important when designing a program for a strength goal to make sure that the exercise selection throughout the cycle will allow for an increase in 1RM average

Here is a 12-week cycle designed to improve the Overhead Press of an online client. The goal of this training cycle was to get close to a 1RM of 225 lbs (102 kg).

Accumulation 7 - 12,10,8,8
Intensification 7 - 5,5,5,9,9
Accumulation 8 - 10,10,8,8,8
Intensification 8 - 6 x 2-4

Exercise Results

DB Overhead Press - Seated - Neutral			
Average Weight	110	Total Weight	440
Average Repetitions	9.5	Total Repetitions	38
Average 1RM	145.3	Total Sets	4
% of Goal Achieved	0	Total Tonnage	4080

BB Overhead Press - Seated - Pronated			
Average Weight	166	Total Weight	830
Average Repetitions	6.6	Total Repetitions	33
Average 1RM	202.9	Total Sets	5
% of Goal Achieved	0	Total Tonnage	5430

BB Behind the Neck Press - Seated - Pronated			
Average Weight	158	Total Weight	790
Average Repetitions	8.8	Total Repetitions	44
Average 1RM	206.1	Total Sets	5
% of Goal Achieved	0	Total Tonnage	6940

BB Overhead Press - Standing - Pronated			
Average Weight	193.3	Total Weight	1160
Average Repetitions	3	Total Repetitions	18
Average 1RM	210.4	Total Sets	6
% of Goal Achieved	93.5	Total Tonnage	3435

The exercise progression used went from Seated DB Press to Seated BB Press to Seated BB Behind the Neck Press and Finally the Standing BB Press.

Granted these exercises are different even though they are all an Overhead Press variation, but notice how the 1RM average goes up from phase to phase.

49

Acc 7 - 145.3 (the weight of both DB's together)
Int 7 - 202.9
Acc 8 - 206.1
Int 7 - 210.4

It is important when designing a program for a strength goal to make sure that the exercise selection throughout the cycle will allow for an increase in 1RM average. Obviously, the rep scheme used will have a huge impact on this as well, but even though the reps were periodized in an alternated fashion, the exercise selection still allowed for a linear progression of the 1RM average.

Another important factor is for the last phase to be the one with the least amount of tonnage (for that lift). At this point, you want to make sure you take precaution at overloading the CNS with extensive loading.

Acc 7 - 4080
Int 7 - 5430
Acc 8 - 6940
Int 8 - 3435

Based on experience, the last phase, you want to aim for a tonnage that is half the one of the previous phase.

By the end of this cycle, the client was able to get to a 1RM of 215 lbs (98 kg) at 93.5% of the goal.

Q: Did you or they have any other goals this phase? Or simply OH press 1RM?
A: I will typically focus on one main upper body goal and one main lower body goal for each 12-week cycle. That's not saying I'm not trying to improve other lifts but the focus as far as the assistance exercises will be around improving the lift

goal. For example, if I'm trying to improve the Pull-up, I would use more exercises that target the brachioradialis for arm work.

Q: Is it ok for that great of a discrepancy in reps as you have in accumulation 8 and intensification 8?
A: Certainly, it's only an 11% spread. Also, keep in mind that more advanced lifters can tolerate bigger contrasts of intensities.

Q: 11% by average 1RM?
A: Exactly, if you average out the % of 1RM of the Acc 8 you have 77% and Int 8 you have 88%.

Strategy 30: The more volume a trainee can tolerate as defined by [Reps x Sets x Number of Exercises x Tempo] the greater the potential for mass gain

Training volume is one of the key triggers to muscle hypertrophy. The more volume a trainee can tolerate as defined by [Reps x Sets x Number of Exercises x Tempo] the greater the potential for mass gain.

Volume is only part of the story. Volume alone cannot lead to optimal hypertrophy, it needs to be combined with load to create adequate muscle damage.

Load is simply the amount of weight on the bar. In essence, you need to combine volume (total reps) and load (total weight) to create the perfect hypertrophy stimulus.

In strength training circles, this concept is referred to as total tonnage. To maximize the training effect, there are tonnage targets to achieve for the perfect training session.

Body part split:
Arms & Shoulders - 10,000 to 15,000 lbs (4,545 to 6,817 kg) per session

Lower Body - 20,000 to 25,000 lbs (9,090 to 11,363 kg) per session

Chest & Back - 15,000 to 20,000 lbs (6,817 to 9,090 kg) per session

There will be times where the total tonnage will be lower and times where it will be higher; this is fine as long as the average of the training cycle falls within these targets.

Q: I assume these numbers change based on a person's training age as well?

A: Not necessarily because of the inverse relationship between intensity and volume. As your training age increases and your intensity goes up, the volume will go down in the end, on average, the tonnage will be similar.

Q: I am guessing these tonnage numbers would decrease as your goal became more relative or Functional Hypertrophy?

A: That's the thing; they would not really. In a hypertrophy phase, you usually have more assistance exercises in the program, like flies, row to neck, etc., In a relative strength phase, you will have multiple sets of heavy deads or squats, etc., because of this, even though the reps are lower, because the nature of the exercise selection and the load they require, in the end it is still about the same tonnage. But like anything in life, there are exceptions.

Q: Do the same numbers apply for female trainees?

A: It would be towards the lower-end of the ranges.

Q: Where do these numbers come from?

A: This was first brought up by Eastern Bloc coaches as a way to evaluate the training sessions of their Olympic lifters.

Later on, bodybuilders started to adapt this system, most notably Chuck Sipes. More recently (late 90's) John Little and Peter Sisco adapted the tonnage system for their Power Factor Training.

Strategy 31: Understanding the strength curve of an exercise allows you as a coach to implement strategies to optimize force distribution throughout the entire range of motion

Understanding the strength curve of an exercise allows you as a coach to implement strategies to optimize force distribution throughout the entire range of motion.

There are three different types of strength curves:

Ascending Curve

The force output increases towards the end of the movement, making the end range the easiest part of the lift (Bench Press).

Descending Curve

The force output decreases towards the end of the movement, making the end range the hardest part of the lift (Chin-up).

Bell Curve

The force output fluctuates throughout the range of motion, making the beginning and the end part of the lift the easiest and the mid range the hardest (Biceps Curl).

A technique that I like for Curls is the use of an isometric pause (2 to 4 seconds) during the concentric contraction. Pausing in the mid range of the curl will increase the force output and the time under tension when the muscle is in its weakest position.

This strategy can be used in situations where there is a need to break a strength plateau or in cases where optimizing complete hypertrophy of the muscle is a priority.

Strategy 32: When trying to improve the Bench Press, the Dip can do wonders to drive your benching score

When trying to improve the Bench Press, the Dip can do wonders to drive your benching score.

Let's examine a progression designed to improve the Bench Press 1RM:

Accumulation 1 - 8-6-6 (Doublé Tri-sets)
A2 Chest Dip 3 x 4-6 3210 tempo

Intensification 1 - 6 x 2-4
A2 Thick-grip Dip 6 x 2-4 50X0 tempo

Accumulation 2 - 5 x 4-6
A2 Triceps Dip 5 x 4-6 3210 tempo

Intensification 2 - 1/1/1/1/1 (Clusters)
A1 2" Thick-grip Inertia Press 5 x 1/1/1/1/1 22X0 tempo

For the entire training cycle, the Bench Press was only introduced as an Inertia Press during the last phase. The first 3 phases focused on the Dips and assistance exercises.

Notice the variation in tempo from phase to phase, going from a pause in the disadvantageous position to a slow eccentric, then back to the pause in the disadvantageous position to finally, dead stops at the sticking point.

There are also variations in the thickness of the implements in order to recruit different motor units by creating more variety to the Dip exercise.

This periodization plan built around the Dips enabled the client to go from a 230 lbs (104 kg) Bench to a 275 lbs (125 kg) Bench Press.

Q: Was the frequency 2x per week or 1?
A: Once every 5 days.

Q: What are your thoughts on using the overhead press to improve the bench press?
A: I really like the overhead press as well. What will make me choose for specializing on one lift or another for Bench Press improvement will depend on the sticking point of the athlete and/or muscular imbalances.

Q: Can you explain further how you set up the double tri-set?
A: A2 Chest Dip 3 x 4-6 3210 10
A3 DB Press 3 x 4-6 4010 180

Q: What made you decide that focusing on dips would improve the bench?
A: The Dip was actully too high for the trainees Bench. But, based on personal experience, I have noticed that trainees with a sticking point in the bottom of the movement (very close to the chest) will benefit more from increasing the Dip compared to someone with a sticking point higher up (mid-range and up). After the trainee had completed this progression, the sticking point was higher up, next I will need a different approach to keep pushing the bench up, and we will be able to get away from Dips, which will close the gap between the two lifts.

Q: The dips are done on an arm only day? Or, is part of the chest day?
A: It varies depending on the phase. Acc 1 was on a Chest &

Back day and Int 1 and Acc 2 were on an Arm day.

Strategy 33: If a trainee scores poorly on external rotator and scapular-retractor strength, a good approach is to undergo a 12-week training cycle that focuses extensively on rowing exercises

The Chin-up is a widely popular exercise in which many trainees focus on in their training programs.

When someone scores poorly on external rotator and scapular-retractor strength, leading to signs of shoulder instability, the focus of the back workout should be around rowing motions.

The problem with focusing on Chin-ups in the early stages of training with these lifters is that Chin-up variations are internal rotators of the shoulders. This action compounds the strength discrepancy between the internal and external rotators of the shoulders.

A good approach is to undergo a 12-week training cycle that focuses extensively on rowing exercises. During that time, Chin-ups should be avoided.

A good rowing progression combined with adequate work for the external rotators will vastly improve shoulder girdle stability, which in return, will greatly help your Chin-up performance once it's reintroduced in the training program.

Q: On this specific case would you stop any pressing movement for chest to emphasize rotator and trap 3 work?
A: In an extreme case I would, but for the most part, limiting the volume of pressing and pausing in the bottom position for a stretch can help. I would also use Fly variations to focus even more on the stretch component.

Strategy 34: When a training cycle is too stagnant or repetitive in style, results will suffer as boredom becomes inevitable

When a training cycle is too stagnant or repetitive in style, often results will suffer as boredom becomes inevitable.

A good approach at this point is to use a phase that is completely different. Doing so will not only make the training experience exciting again, but it will also force the body to adapt to a new stimulus.

A method that is quite interesting for this purpose is to use 2 big lifts per session. Choose one Lower Body and one Upper Body exercise, for example, Snatch-grip Deadlift on Podium and Incline Bench Press.

As far as the loading goes, you want to use 80% of 1RM (7RM) and go for sets of 2 reps only. You go back and forth between the 2 exercises using as much rest as needed. The goal of the first session is to reach 15 sets for both exercises.

As you progress from session to session, you keep the same load but increase the sets and try to reach 30 sets per exercise by the time the training phase ends.

The key is always to complete the workout within the one hour mark. For this type of training, the loading parameter used for progress is density, which is more work done per unit of time.

Because the load is still relatively high (80%) and the volume can reach up to 60 reps per lift, you'll notice gains in muscle hypertrophy.

The muscle fibers targeted are mostly the type IIb and IIx fibers, making this method suitable for the athletic population as well.

Q: How would you set up the rest of the week for this particular training phase?
A:
Monday:
A1 Front Squat
A2 Chin-up

Tuesday:
A1 Snatch-grip Deadlift on podium
A2 Incline Bench Press

Wednesday:
Off

Thursday:
A1 Back Squat
A2 Pull-up

Friday:
A1 Snatch Pulls
A2 Push Press

Saturday:
Off

Sunday:
Off

Strategy 35: Variations in speed of movement during the off-season will yield greater strength gains

With the athletic population, it's important to make sure the athlete is subjected to different speeds of contractions. The rate of force development has to be specific to the sport, but variations in speed of movement during the off-season will yield to greater strength gains than training at a single speed throughout the entire preparation of the athlete.

Here is an example of a football player's off-season progression on the Bench Press:

Accumulation 3
A1 DB Press 1 1/4 reps 5 x 6-8 4010 90

Intensification 3
A1 2" Thick Bar Inertia Press 6,6,4,4,2,2 22X0 120

Accumulation 4
A1 Bench Press with Chains 4,5,6,7,8 30X2 120

Intensification 4
A2 3" Thick Bar Bench Press 3,2,1,3,2,1 20X0 120

Notice how both accumulation phases use a 5-second tempo, but the rate of force development is completely different. In Accumulation 4, the concentric is explosive to teach the athlete to accelerate through the accommodating resistance provided by the chains and the 2-second pause on top allow to tap into higher threshold motor units by allowing partial regeneration of the ATP-CP energy substrates.

In the Intensification 3, the Inertia Press teaches the nervous system to accelerate a load from a dead stop position (very important in football) by using a 2-second pause on the pins. This pause takes out about half of the elastic energy produced during the eccentric phase making the concentric much harder to perform.

In Accumulation 3, the 1 1/4 rep technique is used to strengthen the bottom part of the range of motion by adding time under tension at the weakest point of the lift. This is a good approach in a phase that precedes the use of the Inertia Press as the lift starts from the mid range and the bottom range won't be trained.

Finally, Intensification 4 becomes the fastest phase by using an explosive concentric and an eccentric contraction time that will allow for plenty of elastic energy to build up.

Using this periodization model to speed of contraction will result in greater strength gains than if a constant speed was used.

Q: What the depth is you suggest?
A: In most cases I like to do Inertia Press at about 4 inches from the chest. It would also vary depending on the athletes' sticking point on his bench (if my focus is purely to drive up his bench numbers) or the sports demands, i.e., MMA can require close range Inertia strength, in which case, I would pause closer to the chest.

Q: Are Accumulation/Intensification and so on are all done in separate phases and roughly how long are they lasting?
A: Correct and each phase is 3 weeks in duration.

Strategy 36: By exposing the trainee to various exercises for Posterior Chain development, gains will happen faster as a larger group of motor units are targeted

Posterior Chain development is key in improving an athlete's speed as well as making their physique look powerful.

Let's examine a progression aimed at increasing the hypertrophy of the Posterior Chain:

Accumulation 1* - Supersets

Session 1 & 4

A1 Lying Leg Curl 5 x 6-8 4010 10
A2 Wide Stance Goodmorning 5 x 10-12 3110 180

Session 2 & 5

A1 Lying Leg Curl Feet-in 5 x 6-8 4010 10
A2 Snatch-grip Romanian Deadlift 5 x 10-12 4010 180

Session 3 & 6

A1 Seated Leg Curl 5 x 6-8 4010 10
A2 Horizontal Back Extension 5 x 10-12 3011 180

*For this phase, the Posterior Chain will be trained every 5 days.

This program allows the trainee to train both functions of the hamstrings; knee flexor and hip extensor. The knee flexor is more fast twitch, so the reps are kept at 8 and the TUT at 40 seconds. The hip extensor tends to be slower twitch, so it will come second in the superset and the reps will be higher at 12 with a TUT of 60 seconds.

This progression centers on the variation in the points of loading of the hip extensors. Session 1 & 4 focuses on the lower range of the strength curve with gravity exerting forces when the torso is in the bottom position. Session 2 & 5 targets the mid range with the RDL and session 3 & 6 hits the end range with the Horizontal Back Extension.

Notice how the Leg Curl complements the hip extensor exercise. Session 1 & 4, when the emphasis of the hip extensor movement is on the stretch of the medial hamstring with the wide stance and the pause in the bottom position, the Leg Curl exercise stays very basic in its style and execution. In session 2 & 5, when the emphasis is more focused on the semitendinosus and biceps femoris with the RDL, the Leg Curl favors the semimembranosus by turning the feet inwards. In session 3 & 6, when the loading of the hip extensor is at the end range and the stretch component is minimal, the Leg Curl is the seated variation because the Posterior Chain is in a pre-stretched position by having the torso at 90-degree to the legs.

By exposing the trainee to various exercises, the gains will happen faster as a larger group of motor units are targeted.

Q: What do you think of incorporating some GHR?

A: It's an option for sure, but personally I like to use the GHR in Intensification phases or during a Specific Preparation Phase. The reason I like the Leg Curl better for this situation is the versatility it allows for foot positioning, as well as a more even distribution of forces throughout the entire range of motion with the cam readjusting the strength curve.

Strategy 37: In order to optimize strength and mass gains, the average training intensity of each training cycle has to increase over time

I had a client who visited me to undergo a 7-day Internship. He was looking to improve on his program design knowledge and to apply the new found knowledge on himself.

During the week, we ended up creating his entire year of training. Each workout for the next 52 weeks was now fully prepared and carefully structured.

Here is an overview of the training year:

Cycle 1 - Structural Balance - 12 weeks (3-week phases)

Acc 1 3 x 10-12
Int 1 4 x 6-8
Acc 2 4 x 8-10
Int 2 5 x 4-6

1 Week Off

Cycle 2 - Absolute Strength - 12 weeks (3-week phases)

Acc 3 4 x 7-9
Int 3 7,7,5,5,3,3
Acc 4 8,8,8,6,6
Int 4 5,4,3,5,4,3

1 Week Off

Cycle 3 - Hypertrophy - 12 weeks (3-week phases)

Acc 5 Giant Sets
Int 5 8,8,6,6,4,4
Acc 6 Tri-sets
Int 6 5 x 5

1 Week Off

Cycle 4 - Relative Strength - 12 weeks (2-week phases)

Acc 7 7,5,3,7,5,3
Int 7 5,4,3,3,4,5
Acc 8 6 x 2-4
Int 8 1,6,1,6,1,6
Acc 9 5,3,5,3,5
Int 9 5,4,3,2,1

1 Week Off

Let's look at the data:

3/9/2015

Body Weight: 178 lbs (81 kg)
Bench Press: 285 lbs (129 kg)

Cyclo 1

avg sets per session: 21
avg reps per session: 9
avg intensity: 76%

6/8/2015

body weight: 185 lbs (84 kg)
Bench Press: 320 lbs (145 kg)

Cycle 2

avg sets per session: 23
avg reps per session: 6
avg intensity: 83%

Cycle 3

avg sets per session: 30
avg reps per session: 7
avg intensity: 80%

Cycle 4

avg sets per session: 20
avg reps per session: 4
avg intensity: 88%

3/7/2016

Body Weight: 207 lbs (94 kg)
Bench Press: 405 lbs (184 kg)

Training Year

avg sets per session: 24
avg reps per session: 6.5
avg intensity: 82%

Q: In his case what was the main goal/improvement of the structural balance Phase? What was the average number of sessions per week?

A: For the Lower Body, the main focus was on re-establishing range or motion and improving posterior chain strength. For the Upper Body, the focus was on strengthening the rotator cuffs and scapular-retractors. He scored very low in his evaluation, hence why we dedicated an entire cycle to Structural Balance. He trained 4 to 5 times per week.

Q: What was the goal? Size or strength?

A: Both.

Strategy 38: To expedite full development of the vastus medialis, you want to train it in the top range, the mid range, and the bottom range

Knee injuries are common in many sports in which contact or quick change of direction occurs.

During early stages of the General Preparation Phase, paying attention to muscles surrounding the knee joint can help reduce the risk of injury.

Here is an example of a Lower Body session aimed at improving knee stability:

A1 Petersen Step-up 3 x 10-12 1010 10
A2 Front Foot Elevated Split Squat 3 x 6-8 4010 60
A3 One-leg Lying Leg Curl 3 Positions* 3 x 6-8 5010 60

B1 Front Step-up 3 x 12-15 2010 60
B2 Standing Leg Curl 3 Positions* 3 x 6-8 5010 60

C 45-Degree Back Extension 3 x 10-12 3012 90

D One-leg DB Standing Calf Raise 3 x 10-12 2111 30

* 3 Positions: set 1 - Feet-in, set 2 - Feet-neutral, set 3 - Feet-out

The vastus medialis is important for tracking of the patella, in order to expedite full development of this muscle, you want to train it in the top range (Petersen Step-up), the mid range (Front Step-up) and bottom range (Front Foot Elevated Split Squat).

Supersetting the Pertersen Step-up with the Split Squat allows training the vastus medialis at the opposite end of the spectrum (top and bottom range).

Because the Petersen Step-up requires balance and coordination, it is advisable to keep the reps at a moderate level and to do it first in the session.

The hamstrings are important muscles aiding knee stability. Training the knee flexor unilaterally has the benefit of correcting any potential imbalance between the left and right side, which is why both Leg Curls are done one leg at a time. The use of the 3 Positions technique permits emphasized recruitment of the semimembranosus, semitendinosus and biceps femoris. The reason two different Leg Curls are used is to change the motor unit recruitment pattern of the hamstrings and increasing the exposure to the lift.

The gastrocnemius crosses the knee joint and serves as a knee stabilizer as well. Using the one-legged version will help reduce any potential imbalances as well as increase neural drive to the muscle.

Doing this program will greatly improve co-activation of all the muscles involved at the knee joint.

Q: What would you suggest about a knee moving in during eccentric and the trainee experiencing pain medially at the patella (unilateral)?

A: Start with concentric only work at high volumes with Petersen Sled Drags. After a phase of doing this, reassess the eccentric on Petersen Step-ups.

Q: Why Peterson over Poliquin Step-Up? When do you favor one over the other?

A: They are both great exercises. The Petersen is simply a progression from the Poliquin Step-up. Start with the Poliquin if the client has never done this type of exercise, but as the trainee gets better, the Petersen will present a better challenge as it requires more balance and stability.

Strategy 39: With a strength and power athlete looking for muscular hypertrophy, the training program has to prioritize hypertrophy of the type IIb fast-twitch fibers

In recent years, constant tension sets have been greatly promoted for hypertrophy in bodybuilding circles.

The use of continuous tension creates an oxygen depth to the muscle causing an hypertrophy response primarily in the type I slow-twitch fibers. This adaptation will improve sarcoplasmic hypertrophy response by stimulating the accumulation of glycogen to the muscle cell.

Notwithstanding its effect on hypertrophy, for an athlete looking to increase muscle mass during the off-season, a different approach from continuous tension sets could deem more appropriate. With a strength and power athlete looking for muscular hypertrophy, the training program has to prioritize hypertrophy of the type IIb fast-twitch fibers.

One technique used to neutralize the oxygen depth caused by continuous tension sets is the use of intra-set pauses. By adding a 1 to 2 second pause in the advantageous position of a lift (i.e., at the top of a Bench Press), you allow for partial replenishment of ATP-CP in the muscle cell, enabling the use of higher threshold motor units for the following rep.

For example:

Continuous tension

A Bench Press 4 x 10-12 4010 120

Advantageous position Intra-set pauses

A Bench Press 4 x 6-8 4012 120

Notice how both examples, irrespective of the rep count, almost have the same set duration (60 versus 56 seconds) but the exposure to the set is quite different. While the first example will increase lactic acid output making it almost impossible for the fast-twitch fibers to fire, the second option will engage the CNS to recruit the fast-twitch fibers on every rep.

Both types of hypertrophy have its place in training, but the key is using the method best suited in time for the goals of the trainee.

Q: Is the pause in the advantageous position a passive pause or an active pause where your flexing at the top position?

A: It will be "active" in the sense that stabilizing an 8RM in the lockout position of a Bench Press will require activation and tension. But there is no voluntary squeezing or flexing of the muscles.

Strategy 40: When introducing Wave Loading for the first time, use a smaller intensity spread

Wave Loading is a great method. It is used to disinhibit the nervous system in an effort to allow for heavier loads or more reps at a given intensity, as well as a mean to improve rate of force development (explosive strength) at a given load.

With repeated exposure to Wave Loading, large variations in load can be more beneficial to elicit a training response. For example:

5,3,2,5,3,2

This rep scheme spreads over almost 10%, with 5 reps (85%), 3 reps (90%) and 2 reps (94%).

Training is about progressive overload over a period of time. Using the most advanced methods too early in the training age of a lifter will diminish long term progress.

When introducing Wave Loading for the first time, using a smaller spread can be more effective. For Example:

5,3,5,3,5

This rep scheme spreads over 5%, with 5 reps (85%) and 3 reps (90%).

The trainee will still have the benefits of neural disinhibiting mechanisms, but without the challenge of going through a wide range in intensity spread.

Another important factor is doing fewer sets initially and add more as you progress over time.

As the training age increases, moving to a more challenging Wave will become more effective.

Q: What percentages would you use for 3,2,1 wave loading?
A: 90.6%, 94.3%, and 100%, but I just want to add something I did not touch on in the post. The first wave potentiates the second. These percentages would apply to the last wave, but the first one would be just a bit lower.

Depending on the level of the athlete it could be anywhere from 2 to 5% less for the first wave.

Strategy 41: It is important to understand that the Deadlift works the Posterior Chain as a whole, making exercise selection crucial for fast strength gains

An effective approach to fast strength gains is to train the Lower Body twice within a training week.

An appropriate training split would be:

Monday: Chest & Back
Tuesday: Lower Body
Wednesday: Off
Thursday: Arms & Shoulders
Friday: Posterior Chain
Saturday: Off
Sunday: Off

The Tuesday Lower Body session will focus on a Squat variation and a Lunge or Split Squat variation. On the other end, the Friday session will focus on the Posterior Chain. The emphasis of that session will be on a Deadlift variation and a Glute-ham Raise or Leg Curl variation.

Even though each day has a specific dominance (Quad or Hip), the Posterior Chain can still be trained twice; the key is in exercise selection.

The Friday session is Deadlift day followed with some more isolated knee flexor and hip extensor work. At the end of this workout, your lower back should be completely fatigued.

An advanced athlete will not be able to perform at a high level on Deadlift by Tuesday (hence why a Squat variation is prioritized) but the erector spinae should be ready for some isolated work.

It's important to understand that the Deadlift works the Posterior Chain as a whole and that the co-activation of the entire structure is quite draining to the body.

In an isolated structure, the spinal erectors are very slow-twitch (66% type I fibers[1]). The slow twitch muscles tend to

75

recuperate faster than their fast-twitch counterparts. For this reason, to perform an isolated lower back exercise at the end of the Tuesday session will help to improve your Posterior Chain strength at a faster rate.

Typically, on the Posterior Chain day you will use an exercise like a Goodmorning or Romanian Deadlift and on the Lower Body day you will use a simpler lower back exercise like a 45-Degree or Horizontal Back extension.

[1.] Mannion AF, Weberm BR, Dvorak J, et al. Fibre type characteristics of the lumbar paraspinal muscles in normal healthy subjects and in patients with low back pain. J Orthop Res 1997;15:8817.

Strategy 42: When designing a rehab program, it is important to understand the functional nature of the injured muscle

It is not uncommon for athletes to get a hamstring injury during the season. Proper rehab can make an immense difference in the recurrence of future injuries.

When designing a rehab program, it's important to understand the nature of the injured muscle. Recognizing that the hamstrings are fast-twitch muscles involved in deceleration of high forces, the training prescription should reflect that.

Here is an excerpt of a hamstring rehab program used for a football player:

Monday & Thursday
A One-leg Lying Leg Curl 4 x 6-8 4010 90

Tuesday & Friday
A Accentuated Eccentric Lying Leg Curl* 8 x 3 6010 120

* The concentric is done with both legs and the eccentric is done with one leg.

An important point to understand is that the load is adapted to the tolerance of the athlete.

The first workout has a time under tension of 40 seconds using a conventional set and rep scheme, while the second workout has a time under tension of 21 seconds using an eccentric overload method. Both workouts have time under tensions viable to get a response in the appropriate muscle fibers.

A muscle is stronger eccentrically and because of the deceleration properties of the hamstrings, using an eccentric method is beneficial to the rehab process. Because of the higher trauma caused by eccentric contractions, this session is followed by a rest day.

The frequency is kept high because the strength level is low allowing the recovery curve to be faster. A higher frequency also favors the restoration of intra and inter muscular coordination.

Strategy 43: An effective approach to training the shoulders is alternating phases of volume using isolation exercises, with phases of intensity using compound movements

The shoulder is an interesting body part. It is common knowledge that there are 3 heads to the deltoid muscle (anterior, lateral and posterior), but these fibers are divided into 7 segments based on the distribution of its intramuscular tendons.[1]

To optimally develop a muscle, the use of heavy compound exercises are warranted, but providing the trainee with training phases dedicated to isolate a specific area can complement total muscular development.

An effective approach to training the shoulders is alternating phases of volume (Accumulation) using isolation exercises, with phases of intensity (Intensification) using compound movements.

Considering the fact the deltoid is divided into 7 anatomical segments, using isolation exercises through multiple angles will be greatly beneficial.

Here is an example of an Accumulation and Intensification phase for the shoulders:

Accumulation 1 - Giant Sets

A1 Bent-over DB Lateral Raise 3 x 10-12 2010 10
A2 Prone 45-Degree Incline DB Lateral Raise 3 x 10-12 2010 10
A3 Seated DB Lateral Raise 3 x 10-12 2010 10
A4 Supine 60-Degree Incline DB Lateral Raise 3 x 10-12 2010 10
A5 Seated DB Front Raise 3 x 10-12 2010 180

Intensification 1 - 5 x 5-7

A1 Standing BB Overhead Press 5 x 5-7 5010 90

In the Accumulation phase, the deltoid muscle is targeted via multiple planes of movements, favoring the recruitment of a wide range of different muscle fibers.

In contrast, the Intensification phase uses a compound exercise executed in a single movement pattern. The training effect is gained through heavy loads supported by the co-activation of multiple muscular structures assisting the lift.

In summary, for complete hypertrophy development, using both programming approaches in a periodized plan will help reach higher levels of muscularity.

[1.] Sakoma Y, Sano H, Shinozaki N, et al. Anatomical and functional segments of the deltoid muscle. Journal of Anatomy. 2011;218(2):185-190. doi:10.1111/j.1469-7580.2010.01325.x.

Strategy 44: When training the rotator cuff muscles, creating a contrast in humerus position will favor faster strength adaptations

The rotator cuff muscles are very important muscles for stabilizing the shoulder joint.

Poor rotator cuff strength can lead not only to shoulder instability, but also to poor performance in upper body exercises.

Here is an example of a training set up that can rapidly increase the strength level of the rotator cuff muscles:

Accumulation 1

Upper Body

A1 Flat DB Press 4 x 8-10 5010 10
A2 Arm Adducted to Side Mid-pulley External Rotation 4 x 12-15 3010 60

B1 Seated Rope Row to Neck 4 x 8-10 3012 10
B2 Seated Arm Abducted to Side DB External Rotation 4 x 12-15 3010 60

Intensification 1

Lower Body

A1 Incline DB Press 5 x 5-7 4010 15
A2 Arm Adducted at 30-degree Low-pulley External Rotation 5 x 8-10 3010 90

B1 Seated Row to Waist 5 x 5-7 3110 15
B2 Seated Arm Abducted in Front DB External Rotation 5 x 8-10 3010 90

Alternating the primary exercises with a rotator cuff exercise will speed up the training response by insuring you're stimulating the appropriate musculature to stabilize the prime mover.

Furthermore, the rotator cuffs are targeted earlier into the workout and at the same training volume as the primary lifts. This will allow for a better training effect than if they were trained at the end for a limited amount of sets.

Notice how in both phases I use a pulley and a DB exercise for the rotator cuff. With the DB primary lift, I'll use the pulley rotator cuff lift and with the pulley primary lift I'll used the DB rotator cuff exercise. This is mainly to give the trainee a different stimulus in the application of the force curve.

Another important point is that both rotator cuff exercises are done at different extremes of humerus positioning. Accumulation 1 you have the A2 exercise with the arm fully adducted to the body, while the B2 exercise is fully abducted away from the body. In Intensification 1, the A2 exercise the arm is adducted, but at 30-degrees away from the body and the B2, the arm is abducted away but in front of the body.

Creating a contrast in humerus position will favor faster strength adaptations as the muscles will be trained to stabilize the shoulder joint at a broader angle.

Q: What is your preferred set-up for the seated Arm Abducted to Side DB External Rotation?

A: Scott Bench.

Strategy 45: When trying to improve your 1RM on either the Squat or the Deadlift, the focus of the microcycle should be on one or the other

The Squat and the Deadlift are 2 essential exercises to Lower Body development.

You can train them both in a training week to increase hypertrophy and gain general strength.

When trying to improve your 1RM on either the Squat or the Deadlift, the focus of the microcycle (5-7 days) should be on one or the other. Unless the trainee is a beginner, It is very difficult to bring both poundage up in a same training phase.

For the Lower Body, an entire 12-week cycle would be dedicated to either increase the Back Squat, the Front Squat or the Deadlift.

Here is an example of how the exercises would be set up in a 12-week cycle dedicated to improve the Back Squat score:

Accumulation 1

Lower Body

Back Squat

Posterior Chain

Above Knee Rack Deadlift

Intensification 1

Lower Body

Back Squat

Posterior Chain

Below the Knee Rack Deadlift

Accumulation 2

Lower Body

Back Squat

Posterior Chain

Below the Knee Snatch-grip Rack Deadlift

Intensification 2

Lower Body

Back Squat

Posterior Chain

Trap Bar Deadlift

Notice how as the cycle progresses, the range of motion of the Deadlift increases. This allows for the lower back to improve its strength without overtaxing the recovery curve by implementing both a full range of motion Squat and Deadlift.

It's important to understand that throughout the cycle, the Back Squat will vary not only in sets and reps schemes, but also in style and technique. One phase could be a Heel Elevated Back Squat, the next could have Chains added followed by a phase with a 2-second pause in the bottom position.

The key point to increase the 1RM is to avoid overloading both exercises with a full range of motion during the same training week.

Q: Have you noticed pausing at various positions in the eccentric of the dead will put greater emphasis on the back vs the glutes/hamstrings and vice versa?

A: Certainly, but keep in mind that different body types will present different overloads through the movement. Long legs and short torso compared to short legs and long torso will display different levers, affecting which part of the musculature is targeted by the different pauses.

Q: If a client's deadlift is stuck at the mid-range, how would you set up a 12 week cycle to improve 1RM of Deadlift for a female powerlifter with weak hamstrings/glutes. Based on above do you do opposite so Full range deads but different styles with increasing ROM of the squat?

A: I would only use the set-up you are describing with an athlete other than a powerlifter. For a powerlifter the technical component of the lift is too important. To get away from the competitive technique of the lift for a 12-week cycle would be a mistake unless you have a long period of time in between meets.

Strategy 46: When the goal of a training cycle is to increase the Squat, combining twice-a-day training with eccentric methods can be an effective approach

A strong Back Squat is unequivocally the foundation of lower body strength.

When the goal of a training cycle is to increase the Squat, having a phase in which the exercise is trained twice a day can be extremely beneficial.

Eccentric training can be a great way to improve strength levels on a lift. The disadvantage of eccentric training is that it can be very draining for the nervous system.

Combining twice-a-day training with eccentric methods can work extremely well.

Here is an example of a training day for the lower body using twice-a-day training and eccentric work:

AM session

A Back Squat 5,3,3,2,2 40X0 240

B1 Standing Leg Curl 4 x 4-6 40X0 90
B2 Lunge 4 x 4-6 30X0 90

C Romanian Deadlift 4 x 6-8 30X0 120

D Standing Calf Raise 3 x 8-10 2210 60

PM session

A Supra-maximal Eccentric Back Squat 7 x 3 6000 300*

* Start the first session with a load of 100% of 1RM. This method uses a 6 second eccentric only contraction, so the help of 2 spotters would be helpful to rack the barbell back up.

Because the PM session uses an eccentric method that demands loads over the trainee's 1RM, the use of a 5 minute rest period will be needed in order to allow for the nervous system to recuperate.

The timing of this strategy is of the utmost importance.

Deciding when to use both methods together in the training cycle will be the key determinant of the success of the training cycle.

This workout should come in the first Intensification of a 12-week cycle.

The first Accumulation phase will serve at increasing the volume and exposure to the lift. The following phase is when you incorporate the twice-a-day training with the supra-maximal eccentric method. This phase will create such trauma that you will need the remaining phases to allow for a super-compensation effect. If you were to finish the cycle with this set-up, your Squat score would plummet in testing.

Strategy 47: When designing a periodized plan for a sport in which the events share many commonalities in training demands, you should schedule the sessions in a way that minimizes overlap

Strongman is a very interesting sport to program for; implementing an appropriate training schedule that will favor the development of the specific lifts performed at the event, as well as enabling adequate recovery can be a challenging task for the strength coach.

Let's take a look at my online client's preparation for the 2016 United States Strongman Nationals on June 11:

The 5 events for this competition are:

1. Log Clean & Press Every Rep with 240 lbs for Max Reps in 60 seconds
2. Hummer Tire Deadlift with 550 lbs for Max Reps in 60 seconds
3. Fingal Fingers for 5 Flips in 60 seconds
4. Conan's Wheel with 600 lbs for Max Distance in 60 seconds
5. Atlas Stones at 280, 310, 340 and 360 lbs in 60 seconds

The training week is divided into 4 training units:

Accumulation 1

Day 1

Upper Body

Day 2

Lower Body

Day 3

A Log Clean & Press Every Rep
B Fingal Fingers
C Conan's Wheel

Day 4

A Hummer Tire Deadlift
B Atlas Stones

With the weight training program, the goal is to improve the Back Squat by 25 lbs and Overhead Press score by 10 lbs.

Because training the event lift is so draining to the body and the nervous system, the variations in intensities from phase to phase will be more pronounced to help CNS regeneration.

Acc 1 76%
Int 1 90%
Acc 2 80%
Int 2 94%

As the Intensifications have very high intensities (90% +), the Accumulation phases are backed off to 80% or less.

With the Strongman sessions, the exercises are paired together to target the same musculature as much as possible.

Day 3 favors the events with an overhead component (except the Conan's Wheel), which complements the Overhead Press driven weight training session of Day 1.

Day 4 focuses on pulling (Deadlift type of movements) to complement the Lower Body session of Day 2. Because Deadlift motions are quite demanding, the number of exercises is limited to 2 and ideally 2 off days will follow this workout.

When designing a periodized plan for a sport in which the events share many commonalities in training demands, as a coach, you have to do your best to schedule the sessions in a way that minimizes overlap.

Q: For the percentages that you've mentioned, are you assigning a rep range for what you think would fall under that percentage or are you getting percentages from the 1RM?
A: Assumption based on a general 1RM continuum. For example, 5 reps being 85% of 1RM, 10 reps 74%, etc.

Strategy 48: Chin-up and Pull-up variations are without a doubt some of the best exercises to develop functional upper body strength

Chin-up and Pull-up variations are without a doubt some of the best exercises to develop functional upper body strength.

Let's examine how the Chin-up exercise progressed in the training of one of my online clients over the first two training Cycles.

Cycle 1 focused extensively on improving external rotator and scapular retraction strength. The training split was:

Arms
Legs
Off
Torso
Off

Cycle 2 progressed to a different training split as it was recognized that longer rest between the same workouts was needed. The training split was:

Torso
Lower Body
Off
Arms
Posterior Chain
Off
Off

Let's take a look at the Chin-up Periodization of Cycle 2:

Accumulation 3

A2 Mid Neutral-grip Chin-up 5 x 6-8 4010 90*

Intensification 3

A2 Mid-grip Chin-up 1,6,1,6,1,6 40X0 120*

Accumulation 4

A2 Mid-grip Pull-up 7,7,5,5,3,3 4010 120*

Intensification 4

A2 Mid-grip Chin-up 3,2,1,3,2,1 30X0 120*

* The Chin-up or Pull-up variations were always performed on Torso day.

Notice the progression in the numbers:

Acc 3 - 94 kg for 8 reps with a predicted 1RM of 120 kg

Int 3 - 107 kg for 6 reps with a predicted 1RM of 128 kg

Acc 4 - 104 kg for 7 reps with a predicted 1RM of 128 kg

Int 4 - 125 kg for 3 reps with a predicted 1RM of 136 kg

The Pull-up being harder to perform explains why the predicted 1RM was the same in Int 3 and Acc 4. That being said, the strength progression used a linear path and the Mid-grip Chin-up improved by 8 kg.

To improve the Mid-grip Chin-up, the exercise was used in both Intensifications to increase exposure to the lift at higher intensities. Furthermore, the 2 Accumulations used the same grip width, but the hand was in a different position, neutral and pronated, instead of supinated in both Accumulations.

Because the average training intensity of Cycle 2 is fairly high (87%) and the trainee had limited experience with low rep training, a simple change in grip position was ample enough to create variety. At this point in time, drastic changes in exercise technique would have been counter productive at driving the Chin-up strength upwards.

Strategy 49: For trainees looking to gain muscle mass and strength, keeping the Accumulation phases at around 6 exercises and the Intensification phases at 4, will help with long term success

Choosing the appropriate number of exercises per session can become perplexing when trying to improve overall strength.

Using too many different exercises can decrease the training response as the motor unit recruitment pool is too vastly dispersed.

To this effect, in the 1960's, Russian weightlifting coach Arkady Vorobyov recommended the use of 2 to 7 exercises per workout, while 4 to 6 being the average.

Here is an example of how the number of exercises per session can be distributed for a 24-week off-season program of an experienced athlete:

General Preparation Phase (4-week phases)

Structural Balance

8 exercises

Accumulation 1

6 exercises

Intensification 1

6 exercises

Specific Preparation Phase (3-week phases)

Accumulation 2

6 exercises

Intensification 2

4 exercises

Accumulation 3

4 exercises

Intensification 3

2 exercises

In the earlier phases, more exercises are needed, as they are isolation-type in nature in order to create a solid general strength foundation as well as correcting muscular imbalances.

As the training progresses closer to the season, more compound exercises are to help carryover strength to the specific needs of the sport.

With higher training intensities, higher amounts of sets are needed to create a training response. With more sets per exercises, invariably, fewer exercises per session can be awarded, as you want to keep your training session within the 60-minute mark.

Generally speaking, for trainees looking to gain muscle mass and strength, keeping the Accumulation phases at around 6 exercises and the Intensification phases at 4, seems to work best for long term success.

Strategy 50: For high-level athletes, you need both the energy systems and the weight training to work in opposites to avoid overlapping of nervous system demands

Training the energy systems is of the utmost importance for high-level athletes.

The careful planning of the energy systems in a cohesive combination with a proper weight training periodization will determine the extent of the success of the off-season program.

Let's take a look at an example of a 12-week off-season weight training periodization for an NHL hockey player:

Accumulation 1

3 x 8-10

Intensification 1

8,7,6,5,4

Accumulation 2

4 x 6-8

Intensification 2

5,4,3,5,4,3

With this weight training plan, let's examine how the energy systems incorporate into the off-season program:

Phase 1

Neural-end Anaerobic Alactic System

40-meter sprints with 75 seconds rest

Phase 2

Metabolic-end Anaerobic Alactic System

100-meter sprints with 4 minutes of active rest

94

Phase 3

Neural-end Anaerobic Lactic System

200-meter sprints with 4 minutes of active rest

Phase 4

Metabolic-end Anaerobic Lactic System

400-meter sprints with 7 minutes of active rest

Notice that contrary to the weight training program, which utilizes alternating periodization, the energy systems are following a linear periodization.

As the athlete approaches the competitive season, the strength and power have to be at their peak, hence finishing the off-season with a wave loading rep scheme.

The energy system development has to be specific to the sport of the athlete, which is why in this case; the off-season ends with the metabolic-end of the anaerobic lactic system.

The key factor to point out is that there is an inverse relationship in volume and intensity when planning both training parameters in a training cycle.

Specifically, as the weight training starts with the most extensive phase prioritizing volume and metabolic components, the energy system prescription exhibits its highest level of intensity and the least amount of volume, and as the training progresses, the opposite occurs.

For best results, you need both training systems to work in opposites, to avoid overlapping of nervous system demands in order to emphasize proper recovery for optimal adaptations.

Q: What would the training split look like with the energy system training and strength training combined? Would you include the energy system training on the same day as a strength session? And would the energy system training go before or after the strength?

A: It could be an Upper/ Lower split with 2-3 energy systems sessions per week depending on the training phase. It really depends on what the athlete's weakest attribute is. If he lacks strength to a greater extent, you would do weight training first and the energy system training 4 to 6 hours after. If he lacks conditioning more than he does strength, than do the energy system session first. In my own experience training NHL players, I've had better success focusing on weights in the AM and energy systems in the PM. Another important point to consider is that in most cases, I like to do the energy system sessions on the same days as the lower body workouts. Doing so allows for better overall recuperation of the training week compared to spreading everything out and creating a constant burden to the lower extremities.

Q: Some experts tend to start the anaerobic power training only when at least a phase of relative strength is completed in order to take advantage of the SNC potentiation. So they follow the same progression, from volume to intensity, for EST as for strength training. Do you always advise reverse periodization for EST? Or sometimes other approaches work better?

A: It depends on the length of the off-season. For example, with NFL players, the off-season period calls for 24 weeks. I complete the first 12-week cycle of the GPP (finishing with a relative strength program) before I introduce AAP in the SPP phase. Sometimes if the athlete is really out of shape, I will use the last 2 phases of the GPP to introduce aerobic capacity and power before working the anaerobic system. For hockey, the most important energy system is the anaerobic lactic system, for this reason I would always finish with this system. If the GPP were to start with the EST on a volume to intensity continuum as with the weight training, it would mean that by the time the hockey season starts, the last time I worked the lactic capacity system would be 9 weeks prior. Assuming we're using a linear periodization, a detraining effect would occur in the system thats most needed for the sport.

Strategy 51: When starting the training process with a new trainee, it is crucial to determine specific goals over the short and long term

When starting the training process with a new trainee, as a coach, it is crucial to determine specific goals over the short and long term.

As the phases progress, the coach needs to analyze the results of the athlete in order to better gauge the development of the training cycle.

To illustrate this process, let's examine the analysis of the training goals and outcomes of Accumulation 1 of one of my online clients.

The Deadlift is at a 1RM of 191 kg, in order to match the Deadlift strength, the Back Squat has to increase by 15 kg and the Front Squat by 13 kg.

For this reason, the first 12-week training cycle will not feature the classical Deadlift at any point, in order to give a chance for the Squats to catch up.

For the upper body, the Bench Press has to improve by 13 kg. To assist the Bench Press progression, the external rotators of the shoulders and the scapular-retractors will be trained twice per every 5-day microcycle and the Dip will be the main extensor lift of the cycle.

In order to reach the Bench Press goal, the Dip has to improve by 32 kg (which is why this lift is the primary focus).

During Accumulation 1, the Dip improved by 5.5% every workout to end with an increase of 18 kg by the end of the 4th session.

The Dip is now at 14 kg of the target to reach the Bench Press goal.

This is when the analysis becomes a pivotal marker in terms of exercise selection for the next 3 phases.

With 14 kg to go, at 4 workouts per phase, I know the trainee needs an increase of 3.3% per session to reach the target. This target is easily attainable in one phase.

Because the end of the cycle will serve as a testing period for the Bench Press, this lift has to be trained in the last phase in order to regain inter-muscular coordination.

This leaves 2 phases, one in which we need to train the Dip again. Because we just trained the Dip, but still need to train a similar movement pattern, the next phase (Intensification 1) will feature the Decline Bench Press.

Finally, the Accumulation 2 will reintroduce the Dip again to close the strength gap, before finishing with the tested lift in the last Intensification phase.

Q: How do you establish the DL to BS ratio?

A: It's not a perfect ratio by any means, but it's a good indication and a solid base. It's the average of the cumulative data of different old school Olympic Lifting and Powerlifting coaches combined with my own experiences training athletes. I like the ratio I use because it's the average of different styles in techniques as well as body types. Like I said it's not always perfect but it works quite well for assessment and strength progression.

Strategy 52: When working on increasing the athlete's throwing velocity in a game, attention should be spent on increasing the strength of the Incline Bench Press and the strength of the scapular-retractors

Preparing a pitcher for a long baseball season requires a thoughtful approach to program design.

The off-season should focus on strengthening the weak links and the development of the specific muscles involved in the sport.

When working on increasing the athlete's throwing velocity in a game, attention should be spent on increasing the strength of the Incline Bench Press and the strength of the scapular-retractors.

There is a correlation between a trainee's 1RM on the Bench Press and throwing speed.[1] That being said, a baseball pitcher's off-season program should focus primarily on DB pressing movements. The last Intensification phase can incorporate the Bench Press to use as a testing measure of progress.

Another important factor to consider is the importance of scapular-retractor strength in order to maintain high velocities. As the scapular-retractor fatigues throughout the innings, the force generation properties of the rotator cuff muscles become compromised.[2] Specifically, the strength of the scapular-retractors provides a stable base of support for the rotator cuff to produce torque and is also correlated with improved overhead throwing accuracy.[3]

Here is an example of a training session for a baseball pitcher:

Intensification 2

A1 Incline Close-grip Bench Press 5 x 3-5 30X0 120
A2 Sternum Chin-up 5 x 3-5 30X0 120

B1 One-arm DB Cobra 4 x 6-8 30X0 90
B2 One-arm DB Row 4 x 6-8 30X0 90

C One-arm Bent-over Supported Trap-3 Raise 4 x 6-8 30X0 90

[1] Marques, Mário C., et al. "Relationship Between Throwing Velocity, Muscle Power, and Bar Velocity During Bench Press in Elite Handball Players." (2007).

[2] Tyler, Timothy F., et al. "The effect of scapular-retractor fatigue on external and internal rotation in patients with internal impingement." Journal of sport rehabilitation 18.2 (2009): 229.

[3] Patel, Hardik A., R. Arunmozhi, and Umer Arfath. "Efficacy Of Scapular Retractor Strength Training Vs Thrower's Ten Programme On Performance In Recreational Overhead Athletes-A Comparative Study." International Journal of Therapies and Rehabilitation Research 3.1 (2014): 1.

Strategy 53: It is important to identify the ideal stance for an athlete's squat based on their anatomy

A full range of motion Squat is unequivocally key to optimal athletic development.

An issue that is often observed by strength coaches on the technical aspect of the full range of motion Squat is a posterior pelvic tilt (hip tuck or butt wink) towards the bottom position of the lift.

It's important to understand that there is an anatomical perspective to the posterior tilt of the pelvis that affects the biomechanics of the movement.

Individuals with deep hip sockets will have the hip stability to exert great forces at the top range of the Squat, but will have trouble getting into the bottom position. In fact, by going excessively deep, these athletes will be at greater risks of labral tears or femoroacetabular impingement syndrome. With deep hip sockets, as the hip and knees flexes into a deep Squat, the femur bound up with the anterior part of the acetabulum, forcing the pelvis to breakaway and flex the spine; which overtime, can lead to bulging discs.

What is important when assessing the Squat of the athlete is figuring what the ideal stance is for their anatomy. The shallow hip socket trainees will do well with a narrower stance, but the deep hip socket lifters will need a wider stance.

However, as a coach, there are program design considerations you can use to help your client Squat deeper without excessive hip tuck.

Poor dorsiflexion at the ankle and a tight hip structure, including the gluteus, the piriformis, and the adductor magnus can be a major contributor to excessive posterior tilt of the pelvis.

Starting with a 12-week training cycle devoid of any type of

Squatting can be beneficial to help alleviate and correct the stress caused by a pronounced hip tuck.

Here is an example of a Lower Body session designed to help attain a full range of motion Squat:

Accumulation 1

A1 Low-pulley Split Squat 3 x 10-12 4010 60
A2 One-leg Lying Leg Curl 3 x 6-8 5010 60

B1 DB Front Step-up 3 x 15-20 2010 60
B2 Wide Stance Seated Goodmorning 3 x 12-15 3010 60

C Seated Calf Raise 3 x 12-15 2210 60

D Ball Crunch 3 x 10-12 3011 60

Q: Is there a test you use to figure out if one has deep hip sockets vs shallow?
A: The Hip Scour Test.

Strategy 54: Strength gains will occur faster when different modes of contractions are used

Eccentric training can be an extremely powerful method to help break strength plateaus.

Strength gains will occur faster when different modes of contractions are used.

During the training year, eccentric methods should represent 20% of the workload.

With eccentric training, maximal strength will improve through an increase in neural drive and amount of motor units recruited.

An important facet of eccentric work is that the strength gained eccentrically will carryover to concentric strength, making this method particularly efficient at enhancing strength of highly trained athletes.

Here are general guidelines for eccentric training:

1 rep @ 10-second eccentric with 150%* of 1RM for 5 to 7 sets

2 reps @ 8-second eccentric with 140% of 1RM for 4 to 6 sets

3 reps @ 7-second eccentric with 130% of 1RM for 4 to 6 sets

4 reps @ 6-second eccentric with 120% of 1RM for 3 to 5 sets

5 reps @ 5-second eccentric with 110% of 1RM for 3 to 5 sets

* For highly trained individuals, maximum eccentric strength can reach 175% of 1RM

A significant detail to consider when designing an eccentric training session is that females are remarkably stronger than males eccentrically.[1] For this reason, less training volume will be needed to elicit a training response.

48 hours post training, the muscular damage caused by supra-maximal eccentric training methods are increased 5-folds compared to concentric training methods.[2] The full recovery can take up to 120 hours compared to the 72 hours from concentric methods, so an appropriate training split is of the utmost importance.

[1] Hollander, Daniel B., et al. "Maximal eccentric and concentric strength discrepancies between young men and women for dynamic resistance exercise." The Journal of Strength & Conditioning Research 21.1 (2007): 37-40.

[2] Talag, Trinidad S. "Residual muscular soreness as influenced by concentric, eccentric, and static contractions." Research Quarterly. American Association for Health, Physical Education and Recreation 44.4 (1973): 458-469.

Q: Would you say there is a baseline strength level one should achieve before getting into eccentric training in relation to bodyweight?

A: Generally speaking, you need a training age of 2 years and on Squats, you should be able to Full Squat at least 1.5 times body weight before doing supra-maximal eccentric methods. These are only general guidelines as there are other more important factors to consider, like the strength deficit and/or the demands of the sport.

Strategy 55: The obliques and the transverses can be trained adequately when performing heavy compound movements, while the rectus abdominis requires targeted training

Abdominal training is an important component of the off-season training program of an elite athlete.

The abdominal wall contains 4 muscles: external oblique, internal oblique, transverses and the rectus abdominis.

The primary function of the rectus abdominis is to flex the spine and compress the abdominal and pelvic cavities.

The other 3 muscles exert secondary mobilizer functions and contribute significantly to core stability.

The diagonal orientation of the external and internal oblique muscles make them responsible for flexing and rotating the spine while simultaneously supporting the abdomen and pelvis.

The transverse abdominis muscle stabilizes the pelvis when running or throwing.

Because of their core stabilizing properties, the obliques and the transverses can be trained adequately while performing heavy compound movements.

The rectus abdominis is more involved in powerful sporting actions by exerting high dynamic forces.

With the average population, the abdominal wall has a mixed fiber-type ratio[1], but with athletes, the rectus abdominis has denser and higher proportions of fast-twitch fibers.

Because of the nature of the rectus abdominis, exercises that are done with a minimum of 6 reps and a maximum of 15 reps are prioritized.

For this reason, a progressive planning of abdominal work within the General Preparation Phase (GPP) and the Specific Preparation Phase (SPP) will yield the best results.

During the GPP, the early stages will emphasize the work of

the stabilizers, as the compound movements are not yet involved in the programming.

As the training progresses, the abdominal training will shift towards more rectus abdominis work. When first introduced, higher training volumes and slower velocities are prioritized as a baseline for the upcoming dynamic abdominal work of the SPP.

Because the SPP has the athlete preparing for the demands of the sport, the abdominal training has to reflect the specificity in terms of mode of contractions, i.e. faster velocities.

[1] Häggmark, Thorstensson. "Fibre type in human abdominal muscles." Acta Physiologica Scandinavica. Dec;107 (1979):319-25.

Strategy 56: The development of muscular imbalances is common in unilateral dominant sports; paying special attention to the Structural Balance phase is crucial

Outrigger canoeing is an endurance based sport with a repetitive movement pattern. Such a sport has very specific training demands.

A major culprit of this activity is the development of substantial muscular imbalances caused by the actions of the sport.

Let's take a look at the needs analysis of canoeing:

- The stroke is reaching forward with a straight torso and a moderate tilt forward and rotation from the pelvis
- The bottom arm is straight and the upper arm is slightly bent for lateral stability of the paddle shaft
- The blade is planted forward and ahead of the toes, followed by uncoiling and rotation of the torso
- The bulk of the power comes from the transverse abdominis
- There is a secondary engagement from a leg drive and the lats

Let's examine the training of an online client, designed to help him improve on his 3rd place finish from last year at the Hong Kong National Championships:

Sport specific weaknesses of the athlete:

- The upper back has a tendency to collapse at the catch, particularly when fatigue arises
- The abdominal wall does not fully engage, leading to the athlete pulling too much with the torso
- Difficulty with balance at about 15 km or when the water is rough, causing the lower back to compensate
- The gluteus and hamstrings tighten and fatigue considerably after 12-15 km, affecting torso rotation

- Improving strength-endurance in the lats for occasional bursts of power in the later parts of the race

Structural Balance 1

Upper Body

A1 Neck Extension on Ball 3 x 4-6 1018 15
A2 Trap-3 Raise 3 x 10-12 3011 15
A3 External Rotation 3 x 10-12 3011 15

B1 Elbow-out Pulley Row 3 x 8-10 3012 60
B2 Decline DB Press 3 x 8-10 3210 60

C1 Decline DB Pullover 3 x 10-12 3110 45
C2 DB Unrolling Fly 3 x 10-12 3110 45

D1 Low-pulley Curl 3 x 12-15 3010 30
D2 Rope French Press 3 x 12-15 3010 30

Lower Body

A Petersen Step-up 3 x 8-10 1010 60

B1 Split Squat 3 x 8-10 4010 75
B2 Leg Curl 3 x 8-10 4010 75

C1 Goodmorning 3 x 10-12 4010 15
C2 Back Extension 3 x 12-15 3011 15
C3 Hip Extension on Ball 3 x 15-20 3010 180

D Standing Calf Raise 3 x 10-12 2111 15

E Pallof Press 3 x 2-4 10115 15

Q: With the pallof press, would you have the athlete standing or kneeling in this sb phase?
A: Standing.

Strategy 57: When planning for multiple yearly competitions, a good approach is to follow the competitive event with a transition phase that focuses on structural balance

Let's look at an overview of a 6-month periodization of a female powerlifter leading up to a competition:

8/31/2015 - General Preparation 1 - 4 x 4-6

9/28/2015 - Specific Preparation 1 - 6 x 2-4

10/19/2015 - Specific Preparation 2 - 8 x 2-3

11/9/2015 - Peaking 1 - Taper

11/14/2015 - Competition 1 - Provincials

11/16/2015 - Transition 1 - Structural Balance

12/7/2015 - General Preparation 2 - 8,8,6,6,4,4

1/4/2016 - Specific Preparation 3 - 5,4,3,5,4,3

1/25/2016 - Specific Preparation 4 - Cluster

2/8/2016 - Peaking 2 - Taper

2/15/2016 - Competition 2 – Nationals

When planning for multiple yearly competitions, a good approach is to follow a meet with a transition phase that focuses on structural balance.

Strategy 58: A practical way to teach proper lifting mechanics in the Deadlift is using a progression in which the range of motion slowly progresses over time

Form is critical for the Deadlift. The path of the barbell should always be linear and should start over the middle of the foot and stay close to the legs throughout the entire movement.

Having a barbell trajectory in which the load is pulled away from the legs, which pushes the center of mass in front of the body, creates increased compressive forces at the lumbar spine, putting the trainee at risk of spinal injuries.

A practical way to teach proper lifting mechanics in the Deadlift is using a progression in which the range of motion slowly progresses over time.

Here is an example of a Deadlift exercise progression over a 12-week training Cycle:

Accumulation 1
A Mid-tigh Snatch-grip Rack Deadlift

Intensification 1
A Above-the-knee Clean-grip Rack Deadlift

Accumulation 2
A Below-the-knee Snatch-grip Rack Deadlift

Intensification 2
A Floor Clean-grip Deadlift

Notice that as the range of motion increases in a linear

111

fashion, the grip alternates between Snatch-grip and Clean-grip in order to create a more pronounced variation in range of motion throughout the entire movement.

Strategy 59: Training multiple daily sessions are possible, but only when the different training modalities are carefully planned throughout the training week

Steven Jackson, NFL running back, is one of the hardest working athletes I have ever trained and it was a privilege to be a part of his professional career.

As a tribute to his hard work, here is a glimpse into Steven's last weeks of training leading up to training camp in the summer of 2010:

Intensification 4
Week 1

Monday: 6/28/2010
7am - Starting Speed
12pm - Chest & Back
7 pm - Testing Drills

Tuesday: 6/29/2010
7am - Acceleration
12pm - Lower Body
7 pm - Position Specific Drills

Wednesday: 6/30/2010
7am - Tempo Run
12pm - Arms & Shoulders
7 pm - Testing Drills

Thursday: 7/1/2010
7am - Acceleration
12pm - Posterior Chain
7 pm - Position Specific Drills

Friday: 7/2/2010
7am - Starting Speed
12pm - Chest & Back
7 pm - Testing Drills

Saturday: 7/3/2010
Off

Sunday: 7/4/2010
Off

Week 2
Monday: 7/5/2010
7am - Acceleration
12pm - Lower Body
7 pm - Position Specific Drills

Tuesday: 7/6/2010
7am - Tempo Run
12pm - Arms & Shoulders
7 pm - Testing Drills

Wednesday: 7/7/2010
12pm - Active Recovery

Thursday: 7/8/2010
7am - Starting Speed
12pm - Chest & Back
7 pm - Testing Drills

Friday: 7/9/2010
7am - Acceleration
12pm - Posterior Chain
7 pm - Position Specific Drills

Saturday: 7/10/2010
Off

Sunday: 7/11/2010
Off

Week 3

Monday: 7/12/2010
7am - Tempo Run
12pm - Arms & Shoulders
7 pm - Testing Drills

Tuesday: 7/13/2010
7am - Acceleration
12pm - Lower Body
7 pm - Position Specific Drills

Wednesday: 7/14/2010
7am - Starting Speed
12pm - Chest & Back
7 pm - Testing Drills

Thursday: 7/15/2010
7am - Acceleration
12pm - Posterior Chain
7 pm - Position Specific Drills
Friday: 7/16/2010
7am - Tempo Run
12pm - Arms & Shoulders
7 pm - Testing Drills

Saturday: 7/17/2010
Off

Sunday: 7/18/2010
Off

Week 4

Monday: 7/19/2010
12pm - Lower Body

Tuesday: 7/20/2010
12pm - Upper Body

Wednesday: 7/21/2010
Off

Thursday: 7/22/2010
Training Camp...

Training multiple daily sessions are possible, but only when the different training modalities are carefully planned throughout the training week.

116

Strategy 60: Numbers are extremely important when assessing programs for optimal long-term success

Numbers are crucial when assessing programs for optimal long-term success.

Here is an example of the impact programming and numbers have on the ability to reach training goals.

Let's examine the training cycle of a client designed to improve the Squat to a 1RM goal of 225 kg (495 lbs):

Accumulation 1

A Squat 12,12,10,10,8 4010 180

Intensification 1

A Squat 6,4,2,6,4,2 40X0 240

Exercise Results

Back Squat										
Sets	1	2	3	4	5	6	7	8	9	10
Weight	120	122	127	129	130					
Reps	12	12	10	9	8					
1RM	169.8	172.6	171.1	169.3	166					

Back Squat			
Average Weight	125.6	Total Weight	628
Average Repetitions	10.2	Total Repetitions	51
Average 1RM	169.8	Total Sets	5
% of Goal Achieved	75.4	Total Tonnage	6375

Back Squat										
Sets	1	2	3	4	5	6	7	8	9	10
Weight	170	182	196	172	185	200				
Reps	6	4	2	6	4	2				
1RM	204.6	205.3	206.1	207	208.7	210.3				

Back Squat			
Average Weight	184.2	Total Weight	1105
Average Repetitions	4	Total Repetitions	24
Average 1RM	207	Total Sets	6
% of Goal Achieved	92	Total Tonnage	4312

The first 2 charts are from the Accumulation. Notice how the predicted 1RM score decreases as the sets progress.

This response to the training prescription can indicate poor buffering capacities.

The average weight lifted is 125.6 kg (276 lbs) and the predicted 1RM is at 169.8 kg (374 lbs) at 75.4% of the lift goal of 225 kg (495 lbs). The tonnage for the lift is at 6,375 kg (14,025 lbs).

The last 2 charts represent the Intensification 1.

As the trainee is an advanced lifter, using bigger intensity variations from phase to phase challenges the nervous system to a greater extent.

Notice how the predicted 1RM constantly improves from set to set; but this is not surprising as the athlete demonstrated better fast-twitch properties based on the buffering capacities revealed in Accumulation 1.

It's interesting to see that the predicted 1RM went from 169.8 kg (374 lbs) to 207 kg (455 lbs) with 92% of the lift goal of 225 kg (495 lbs) compared to the previous phase at 75.4%.

Even though the total volume is half from what it was in phase 1, the tonnage in Intensification 1 is only a third less at 4,312 kg (9,486 lbs) compared to 6,375 kg (14,025 lbs).

This lifter clearly is more efficient at lower reps than higher reps.

With this information, for the Accumulation 2, the rep scheme will be set at an average rep of 6 (slightly higher than the Intensification at an average rep of 4) to make sure the training program keeps the trainee close to the 225 kg (495 lbs) lift goal.

From the modification of the periodization, learned from the assessment of the workout log, the athlete should reach the goal of a 225 kg (495 lbs) 1RM by the end of Intensification 2.

Strategy 61: When programming for a qualified athlete, variation is important as the nervous system adapts to a stimulus at a faster rate

The Split Squat is a great exercise for functional strength development and to promote dynamic flexibility of the entire lower body structure.

One of my online clients suffered from Femoroacetabular Impigement Syndrome in the left hip that was corrected via surgery. At the moment, the left hip is pain free, but the right hip is symptomatic of pain in deep flexion, as well as deep flexion combined with external rotation.

The training goal is to compete in a decathlon which is a combination of 10 different events ranging from 400 meter runs to maximum Bench Press for reps, etc.

The first lower body training priority is structural balance and range of motion improvement at the hips and ankle.

The major tightness issues of the trainee are in the adductor magnus, the rectus femoris and the hip external rotators.

The Split Squat exercise recruits many muscles; adductor magnus and brevis, vastus medialis, intermedius and lateralis, gluteus, quadrates lumborum, as well as increase the flexibility of the hip flexor, hip external rotators and ankle dorsiflexion.

In order to ultimately prepare the athlete for the Back Squat, the first 2 phases had the lifter perform a Split Squat variation twice a week.

Accumulation 1

Lower Body 1

A1 DB Split Squat Front Foot Elevated 3 x 10-12 3110 75

Lower Body 2

A1 Low-pulley Split Squat 3 x 10-12 3110 75

Intensification 1

Lower Body 1

A1 BB Split Squat 5 x 5-7 3110 90

Lower Body 2

A1 1 1/4 Rep DB Split Squat 5 x 5-7 4010 90

Notice how all the Split Squat variations are different, either a different foot position, a different implement or a different technique.

When programming for a qualified athlete, variation is important as the nervous system adapts to a stimulus at a faster rate. Furthermore, the exercise variety will better prepare the trainee for the diversity of the sporting events.

The client still experiences some bilateral discrepancies with the right side being tighter, as the right hip is still exhibiting discomfort.

Keeping the focus on Split Squats for the next 2 phases should help substantially in correcting the remaining muscular imbalances.

Strategy 62: High levels of maximal strength are extremely important for athletic success, as it is correlated with the ability to apply explosive forces

One of the greatest athletic attributes is the ability to exert maximal forces rapidly.

In strength training, this concept is called the rate of force development (RFD).

High levels of maximal strength are extremely important for athletic success, as it is highly correlated with the ability to apply explosive forces.

The drawback to exerting peak torque through maximal voluntary contractions (MVC) is that it is time dependent.

In activities like jumping or sprinting, maximal strength is a great determinant of performance as the nervous system has time to produce high levels of peak forces before the action is deployed.[1]

With movements characterized by extreme speed, like punching or kicking, maximal strength becomes less relevant as the athlete doesn't have enough time to create high levels of maximal strength.

The efficiency of movements of this magnitude is highly determined by the contractile properties of the muscle fibers.

In fact, the twitch properties of type IIa and IIx fibers are 4 and 9 times faster than type I fibers, so a trainee with predominantly slow-twitch muscle fibers is greatly disadvantaged.[2]

Understanding that to a certain extent maximal strength is a positive determinant of speed, as a coach, the training program needs to use methods and techniques that will enable the lifter to improve the RFD through MVC.

At this point, the goal of the training program is to teach the nervous system to exert high levels of forces at an improved speed.

Techniques focusing on barbell speed and ballistic movements become a priority in order to transfer the training to the sporting event.

One such technique is the use of a myotatic contraction. By using stored elastic energy, the nervous system improves its RFD via increase firing rate of high threshold motor units.

[1.] Schmidtbleicher, Diertmar. "Training for power events." Strength and power in sport 1 (1992): 381-395.

[2.] Bottinelli, R., et al. "Force-velocity properties of human skeletal muscle fibres: myosin heavy chain isoform and temperature dependence." The Journal of physiology 495.2 (1996): 573-586.

Strategy 63: To optimize the training effect, the total duration of a Giant Set should be around 150 to 180 seconds for men and 180 to 210 seconds for women

Well-developed legs are the benchmark of a complete physique.

Generally speaking, the quadriceps have a mixed proportion of muscle fibers.[1]

An important factor in program design is that men tend to have more fast twitch properties in their quadriceps, while women tend to have more slow twitch fibers.[2]

The hamstrings tend to exhibit more fast-twitch properties.[3]

Time under tension, muscular damage, volume, density and motor unit recruitment spectrum are the primary causes of hypertrophy.

Giant Sets are excellent at prolonging the time under tension to the muscle while targeting a large pool of motor units.

Changing exercises allows the trainee to keep higher average levels of tension to the muscle compared to doing a single set of very high repetitions.

Because of the contractile properties of the fibers of the quadriceps and hamstrings, the selection of repetitions will be an important determinant of the effectiveness of the training program.

Here is an example of a Giant Sets session for the lower body:

A1 Back Squat 5 x 6-8 3010 15

A2 Heel Elevated Back Squat 5 x 6-8 3010 15 3010 15

A3 BB Hack Squat 5 x 6-8 3010 15

A4 Hack Squat Machine 5 x 8-10 3010 15

A5 Leg Press 5 x 20-25 1010 120

B1 One-leg Lying Leg Curl, Foot-neutral 5 x 6-8 3010 10

B2 Standing Leg Curl, Foot-in 5 x 6-8 3010 10

B3 Kneeling Leg Curl, Foot-out 5 x 6-8 3010 10

B4 One-leg Seated Leg Cur, Foot-neutral 5 x 6-8 3010 10

B5 High Box Step-up 5 x 10-12 1010 120

To optimize the training effect, the total duration of the Giant Set should be around 150 to 180 seconds for men and 180 to 210 seconds for women.

[1] Johnson, M_A, et al. "Data on the distribution of fibre types in thirty-six human muscles: an autopsy study." Journal of the neurological sciences 18.1 (1973): 111-129.

[2] Staron, Robert S., et al. "Fiber type composition of the vastus lateralis muscle of young men and women." Journal of Histochemistry & Cytochemistry 48.5 (2000): 623-629.

[3] Dahmane, Raja, et al. "Spatial fiber type distribution in normal human muscle: histochemical and tensiomyographical evaluation." Journal of biomechanics 38.12 (2005): 2451-2459.

Q: What is the reasoning for the High Box Step-up at the end of the hamstring giant set?

A: After focusing on the knee flexion function of the hamstrings for 4 exercises, it's a great way to target the hamstrings through the hip extensor function (because of the full range of motion provided by the high box) without overtaxing the lower back that got quite the workout from so much squatting.

Q: Could a split squat also be used in place of a High Box Step-up or should the box be so high it resembles a pistol squat?

A: You would need a high box, but the key will be doing a Step-up with a vertical torso and shin displacement (avoiding leaning forward too much). By doing so, the hamstrings will fire to a greater extent than a Step-up where the torso and knee are going forward (where the quads will become the dominant muscle). A Split Squat would be too quad dominant to get the same effect on the hamstrings and the Pistol Squats also has a forward shin displacement taking some of the hamstrings involvement away from the movement.

Strategy 64: In order to improve a trainee's Incline Bench Press, the General Preparation phase should focus mostly on DB work for pressing movements

The Incline Bench Press is an excellent indicator of overall upper body strength.

In order to improve on this lift, the stabilizers of the shoulders have to be challenged.

The trainee will train the external rotators and the scapular-retractors twice a week during the General Preparation phase and then the frequency will be reduced to once a week during the Specific Preparation phase.

In order to extend the exposure and the recruitment of the shoulder stabilizers, the General Preparation phase should focus exclusively on DB work for pressing movements.

For one workout, the pressing exercise will be a DB Overhead Press variation and for the other upper body session, the emphasis will be on an Incline DB Press variation.

Here is an example of a General Preparation phase progression for the Incline Bench Press:

Accumulation 1

Upper Body 1

A1 One-arm Standing DB Overhead Press 3 x 10-12 4010 60

Upper Body 2

A1 30-Degree Incline DB Press 3 x 10-12 4010 60

Intensification 1

Upper Body 1

A1 Seated DB Overhead Press 5 x 5-7 4010 90

Upper Body 2

A1 45-Degree Incline DB Press 5 x 5-7 3110 90

Accumulation 2

Upper Body 1

A1 Standing DB Overhead Press 4 x 8-10 4010 75

Upper Body 2

A1 60-Degree 1 1/4 Rep Incline DB Press 4 x 8-10 4010 75

Intensification 2

Upper Body 1

A1 Unsupported Back Seated DB Overhead Press 5 x 4-6 4010 120

Upper Body 2

A1 45-Degree Incline DB Press 5 x 4-6 4010 120

Because the testing of the Incline BB Bench Press will be at a 45-Degree angle, that specific angle is trained twice within the 12-week cycle.

Both Accumulation phases are used to train the least specific angles to the tested exercise.

If the testing protocol is based on volume, i.e. max Bench Press repetitions, the exercise should be trained in the Accumulation phases.

If the testing focus is on load (1RM), the exercise should be featured in the Intensification phases.

An important aspect to DB pressing numbers is that the combined weight of both dumbbells should represent 90% of the BB pressing score at the same angle and rep range.

Q: In this example, would you pair the press with a pulling movement on one day and with an elbow flexor on the other day and avoid direct elbow extensor exercises?

A: You could do the Overhead Press with a Chin-up variation and the DB Press with a Rowing variation. The B series would be a biceps or a remedial rowing exercise with a triceps exercise. The C series would be the scap-retractors and rotator cuffs.

To improve pressing exercises, triceps work tends to carryover quite well.

Strategy 65: Incorporate calf work in the training plan of an athlete because a stronger gastrocnemius will aid in stabilizing the knee joint

One of the most underestimated muscles in athletic performance training are the calves.

There are 2 important reasons to incorporate calf work in the training plan of an athlete:

1. Because the origins of the gastrocnemius are at the medial and lateral condyle of the femur and the muscle assists in flexion of the knee, a stronger gastrocnemius will aid in stabilizing the knee joint.

2. Greater ankle dorsiflexion will improve Squatting mechanics, as well as, help decrease the incidence of knee injuries.

It's important to understand the fiber type of each muscle in order to program the appropriate training protocol.

The gastrocnemius and anterior tibialis both have a mixed fiber make-up with an emphasis on fast-twitch properties, while the soleus is predominantly slow-twitch.[1, 2]

In programming, consider that the ankle range of motion needs to be trained both with the knee extended (Standing Calf Raise) and the knee flexed (Seated Calf Raise) in order to have complete transfer to sporting events.[3]

During the Specific Preparation phase, the anterior tibialis should be trained every other program during the Accumulation phase.

When the anterior tibialis is in a fatigued state, the running mechanics are affected. To this effect, the last Intensification phase leading to training camp should be devoid of direct anterior tibialis work.

Here is an example of a calf workout during the General Preparation phase:

C One-leg Standing DB Calf Raise 4 x 8-10 2111 60

D1 Anterior Tibialis Raise 3 x 10-12 2011 10
D2 Seated Calf Raise 3 x 20-25 2010 90

[1] Edgerton, V. Reggie, J. L. Smith, and D. R. Simpson. "Muscle fibre type populations of human leg muscles." The Histochemical journal 7.3 (1975): 259-266.

[2] Yang, Jin Chul, and Joo Yong Yoo. "Histochemical Muscle Fiber Types of Autopsied Human Gastrocnemius, Soleus, Peroneus longus and Tibialis anterior Muscles." Korean Journal of Pathology 20.4 (1986): 413-426.

[3] Fong, Chun-Man, et al. "Ankle-dorsiflexion range of motion and landing biomechanics." Journal of athletic training 46.1 (2011): 5-10.

Q: The reason for the acceleration near the bottom of the eccentric is for elastic benefits?

A: Exactly, this is the myotatic component of the lift.

Strategy 66: In the early phases of the off-season, one way to ensure durability during the competitive season is to address muscle imbalances caused by sport specific actions

With elite level athletes, the initial week of the off-season training period is dedicated to testing the predictor lifts of the sport. Doing so enables the coach to identify any lifts that are out of balance with one another.

One way to ensure durability during the competitive season is to address muscle imbalances, caused by sport specific actions, through the early phases of the off-season.

For the Specific and General Preparation phases, a sound approach is using 3-week training phases that alternate between high volume (Accumulation) and high intensity (Intensification) phases.

Depending on the length of the off-season allowed by the sport, the Specific Preparation and General Preparation phase can last anywhere from 6 to 12 weeks each.

During the General Preparation phase, the nature of the selection of exercises and the average training intensity allows the trainee to recuperate from each training session at a faster rate. With that in mind, using a training split that has a more general set-up is a good strategy.

Here is an example:

Monday: Upper Body 1
Tuesday: Lower Body 1
Wednesday: Off
Thursday: Upper Body 2
Friday: Lower Body 2

Saturday: Off
Sunday: Off

As the lifter progresses to the Specific Preparation phase, the training split needs to be more specific as higher loads, via compound exercises, create a larger dent in the recovery curve. For this reason, more rest between body parts will yield better results.

Here is an example:

Monday: Chest & Back
Tuesday: Lower Body
Wednesday: Off
Thursday: Arms & Shoulders
Friday: Posterior Chain
Saturday: Off
Sunday: Off

Let's take a closer look at a Lower Body and Posterior Chain program design for the Specific Preparation phase of an athlete involved in a power sport:

Lower Body
A Back Squat 6 x 2-4, 40X0 180
B1 Kneeling Leg Curl 4 x 3-5 40X0 90
B2. Drop Lunge 4 x 5-7 30X0 90
C Standing Calf Raise 3 x 8-10 21X0 90
D Med Ball Crunch 3 x 10-12, 30X0 90

Posterior Chain
A Glute-ham Raise 10 x 2-3 40X0 150

B1 Standing Good Morning 4 x 5-7 30X0 15
B2 Snatch-grip Romanian Deadlift 4 x 6-8 30X0 180
C Seated Calf Raise 3 x 15-20 20X0 60
D Hanging Leg Raise 3 x 10-12 30X0 90

During in-season sessions, the volume of training should be reduced significantly in order to allow the athlete to perform at the highest level.

Here are examples of in-season programs for the Lower Body during an Accumulation and Intensification phase:

Accumulation
Lower Body
A Back Squat 3 x 6-8 3010 120
B1 Standing Leg Curl 3 x 6-8 3010 75
B2 Split Squat 3 x 8-10 3010 75
C 45-Degree Back Extension 2 x 12-15 3010 75
D One-leg Standing Calf Raise 2 x 10-12 2010 45

Intensification
Lower Body
A Above-the-knee Rack Deadlift 5,3,3,2 30X0 180
B1 BB Alternated Lunge 2 x 4-6 30X0 120
B2 Lying Leg Curl 2 x 4-6 30X0 120
C Reverse Hyperextension 2 x 8-10 20X0 90

An important consideration for in-season training is avoiding deliberately slow eccentric contractions. Emphasizing eccentric work during the season can negatively affect sports performance as eccentric work creates elevated muscular trauma.

About the Author

Stéphane Cazeault is the founder of KILO.

At the age of 14, Stéphane knew he wanted to be a strength coach. He has spent the last 24 years perfecting his work. He has a strong formal academic foundation, earning a bachelor's degree in exercise science from the University of Montreal. During this time, he worked with mentors to learn the practical skills necessary to enable athletes to achieve physical superiority.

In his career Stéphane has personally trained professional athletes in football, baseball and hockey. Here are some of the athletes he worked with from the NFL, MLB and NHL: Steven Jackson (New England Patriots), James Butler and Mark Clayton (St. Louis Rams); David Freese, Chris Carpenter and Matt Holliday (St. Louis Cardinals); Dennis Wideman (Calgary Flames) and Mike Green (Washington Capitals).

Prior to starting KILO, Stéphane was the Director of Strength and Conditioning for Poliquin Group (2012-2016) and the High Performance Director at the Central Institute for Human Performance (2005-2012).

Stéphane's passion is program design. His program design is carefully structured with every possible component taking into consideration to ensure the trainee reaches and exceeds their goals, making his work a combination of both science and art.

KILO is located in Huntington Beach, California. Visit www.kilostrengthsociety.com for more information regarding services and the KILO Project.

Suggested Reading

Hartmann, Jürgen, and Harold Tünnemann. Fitness and strength training. Sportverlag, 1989.

Komi, Paavo V., ed. Strength and power in sport. Oxford: Blackwell scientific publications, 1992.

Siff, Mel Cunningham. Supertraining. Supertraining Institute, 2003.

Whyte, Gregory. The physiology of training. Elsevier Health Sciences, 2006.

Zatsiorsky, Vladimir M. "Science and Practice of Strength Training. 1995." Human Kinetics, USA: 200-221.

Special Thank You
Members of the KILO Strength Society

Gavin Attore
Guillaume Boucher
Jeffrey Brockes
Steven Collins
Roth Cosner
Barbara Cuddy-Farren
Chris Dellasega
Sarah Evers
Alex Farren
David Fontaine
Hark Gabriel Gil
Chris Garay
Todd Giorgi
Shannyn Hall
Brady Hare
Debbie Huq
Casper Jespersen
Kamay Kan
Sebastien Lagrange
Jean-Marie Lapointe
Craig Lawless
Maikki Marjaniemi
Philippe Massicotte
Alexandre Miranda
Birgitte Moeller Larsen
Sam O'Sullivan
Annie Ragan
Troy Reynolds
Christopher Rombola
Abigail Savage
Brian Schweitzerhof
Nadine Shaban
Aikaterini Stratoudakis
Eugene Teo
Antonio Valverde
Jessica Velarde

To everyone who participated and provided their questions on my social media platforms

Printed in Great Britain
by Amazon